Science and

spirituality

an alliance starting

from

the big bang

Traveller, there are no paths, paths are created by walking.

Antonio Machado

Science and spirituality: an alliance starting from the big bang

a life journey

Johan Germonpré

English text correction: Boudewijn Verhelst and Paul Bentley
Cover design 'Big bang': Nele Germonpré
Dutch edition 2022
English edition 2023 ISBN 9789464857795
Original title: wetenschap en spiritualiteit: een verbond vanaf de oerknal (1st and 2nd print 2022, 3th print 2023)

Content

You can see photos on my website www.scienceandspirituality:

To my wife Christine,

For my children and grandchildren,

and because it's necessary for the earth.

Our spirituality is a unity and interconnectedness with everything that lives and breathes, even with everything that does not. (Aborigines)

What is the purpose of all that? Evolution of consciousness in the small (our own lives) and the big (the cosmos).

This book is intended for everyone, including those who are not scientifically educated!

If you browse through this book quickly, you get the impression that it is scientifically very difficult. But it isn't.

Chapters 1 and 2 are a general introduction.

In *Chapter 3*, we discover through classical natural science that the large universe and the tiny atom are built in a very similar way.

This is followed in *chapters 4 and 5 by* the two new theories (relativity theory and quantum mechanics) who put all the foregoing in a new light.

Simple summaries follow under the title 'briefly summarised' after chapters 3, 4, 5, 6, 7, 11 and 12. So don't worry if you do not understand everything immediately. These summaries are sufficient to continue reading the book.

You can also just go through those summaries after the first two chapters and browse a bit and read some travel dialogues as your first exploration of this book.

In *Chapter 6,* we notice that a living creature does not just behave according to classical laws of nature. Life cannot exist without the 'bizarre' quantum mechanics.

Chapter 7 shows that consciousness is present in everything and guides the entire evolution of the universe and the earth.

In *Chapter 8,* you will read how the passing on of life over many generations occurs through the very stable DNA. Exceptional changes in that DNA (mutations) are not just a coincidence.

Now that we understand the engine of evolution a bit, we review in *chapters 9 and 10* (very briefly) the evolution of the animal kingdom. Six laws of evolution appear.

The miracle of human 'thought' is a logical step in the evolutionary process of consciousness. *Chapter 11* demonstrates this and then gives a concise summary of the six laws of evolution.

In *chapter 12,* we also discover those 6 laws of evolution in the history of mankind and then finally in *chapters 13, 14 and 15* we see a wonderful future for mankind through those laws.

Try to read the scientific pieces with your full attention and pick up what is possible. Repeat until you fully understand everything, find more explanations on the internet because then you don't have to accept the context from me. Everything you see for yourself sets you free.

Many interesting topics I only briefly touch upon.... Each of them often deserves a separate study. I hope to titillate your curiosity!

The scientific explanations are sometimes somewhat simplified in order not to go into details when irrelevant to the whole.

Enjoy reading!

Chapter 1

A quest I became aware of in Pakistan

1. Introduction

2 August 2006, Peshawar, northern Pakistan

We are travelling for one year. Christine, my wife, and I. We drive from home, in Belgium, with our car through Turkey and Iran to Pakistan. Eventually, we end up in Peshawar.

While our car is stuck in a flock of sheep, we are approached by an elderly shepherd:

- Which religion do you have?

- I have no religion...

- Are you a communist?

- No, I don't have a religion.

- You don't believe in God?

- I don't believe in the God of religions.

- So who made this world?

- Science can explain this much better than religion!

- Everyone can see that God made the world...

I look into the old man's deep brown eyes. The sun forms a mystical aura around his figure. The deep grooves in his face and around his eyes show a hard and difficult life, but his eyes are pools of softness and compassion. He wants to convince me of nothing, because he 'knows' from his heart. Time suddenly stands still for a moment. Something vibrates inside, down to below my ribs... Words, explanations...? A smile. It touches me deeply. He knows, feels... something I don't know. His views are not theories to him, but they are facts with as much meaning as the reality around him.

In that unimaginable bustle and heat, reality quickly takes over. Honking, we drive on towards the city centre. The seed has been planted...

15 years later, 12 May 2021 Cebreiro, Spain
I am walking on the Camino Francès, towards Santiago de Compostella*.(*=glossary at the back) The first corona lockdown is just over and it feels good to be back on the Camino.

> **In July 1993**, 28 years ago, I came on the Camino for the first time. With my eldest son, a sporty bike ride. Actually, I thought with my 14-year-old teenager France was far enough. But after strong insistence (and a 14-year-old adolescent knows what insistence is!) I gave in to cycle on in Spain after all. It went like this:
> A neighbour had warmed Koenraad to the Camino. On a sunny day, we cycle to Zevenkerken Abbey in Bruges,

looking for info on the bike ride to be made. We ring the bell.

- Hello, is the Father, responsible for the 'Camino de Santiago', present?
- Oh well, I don't know...
- Hey dad, that looks nice here. You can go and stand whenever and wherever you want. It would be something for me....

After some waiting, the priest appears.
- So you want to go on a pilgrimage to Santiago?
- Well, let's say...
- Hoh, how nice! You know, you will pass 'cruz de ferro'.
- And what is 'cruz de ferro'?
- You are supposed to bring a stone with you on your journey. That stone symbolises your sins and shortcomings. If you find that you carry a lot of sins with you in life, you can carry a big stone... And at the top of the last mountain range before Santiago, it's time to leave those shortcomings behind and throw the stone you brought at that stone heap. You can't believe how huge some of the stones are! Tens of kilometres around you will not find a single stone...
(I immediately think of a very small stone to carry that far by bike. Hum. Later, when we pass 'Cruz de Ferro', the stone heap was much smaller than in my imagination. There were also stones not that far away.)

- Yes, but we would not be cycling in Spain, but in France. The 'Camino' runs there too, doesn't it?
The priest looks at the sky and pretends to study a spot on the ceiling very intensely:
- Yes, but the Spanish part is much more beautiful...!
Koenraad nods his head off his neck behind the Father's back*: 'I've been saying it all along!!!'*
I give in, we leave Saint-Jean-Pied-de-Port, France....

Two months later, we drove in about 9 days from Saint-Jean-Pied-de-Port (French Pyrenees) to Santiago de Compostella. Nice weather, it went well, everything a father could wish for with his eldest son. Nothing special you would think. But on 8 July 1993, the last evening of our trip, I note:
It's already 9.30 p.m. We're tired. It has been quite a journey. The city lies ahead of us, seen from the Monte do Gozo. The towers sparkle in the evening sun. Along the narrow, worn-out pilgrims' streets, we drive up the last hill in the city centre. As we rumble our racing bikes on those medieval flat stones, a very intense feeling flows through me: I feel connected to the joys and sorrows of the many thousands of pilgrims before me. Tears spring into my eyes. Everything is wonderful and beautiful. We pass under the last bridge to the cathedral. I see Christine and fall into her arms, sobbing. From happiness. Only later do I realise: this is not only a bike route! There's more to this, but you can't put that 'more' into words....

In November 2000 (7 years later), I found myself back on the route by 'coincidence'.

After the summer holidays, I would just go back to work. But the machine sputtered. Things were no longer spontaneous. That first week of September I stood in front of the classroom with a cardboard head and thought: Is this all? Is this life now? Do I have to keep this up for another 20 years? And then crawl into my coffin several years later?

I watched the sun set on the beach of Zeebrugge and knew that my old life was also going down. The next morning, I resigned at school and decided to look for another job.

I had countless questions and really didn't know what to do with my life. Another job? Move abroad? But what if my family doesn't follow me?

A few days later, while working in our vegetable garden, during that difficult, chaotic period, that moment on the Camino in 1993 with my eldest son came back to my mind. My heart began to beat faster: *'THERE I might find an answer...!'*

A week later, I left Saint-Jean-Pied-de-Port again, in the twilight with a rising November sun. But this time alone. And on foot. With my tent, to be alone with my heavy heart in nature.

And I was indeed given an answer. By the most beautiful thing in that nature: man. By one single conversation on the way to the heights of Cebreiro.

- Today my eldest son died 2 years ago, he had an accident while trekking in the mountains.

- How terrible...

- Yes, and he had a very difficult life too. I can't talk to my husband about it because everything is so painful. That makes it extra heavy to carry...

- I understand that.

- His life has been chaotic and turbulent at times. His walk of life was controversial to the people around us in Le Puy, where I live. But in recent years, he had found peace.

I listen to the boy's life story. But hello!... The mother is not telling her son's life but mine! And right away with the solution. It hits like a bomb. I know immediately that it's correct: by changing external things, you don't change anything. You don't become happier. You think you have solved the difficulties by changing your job, partner, country, but everything remains the same. The real change, the real journey happens inside....

So a few months later, I resumed my work with renewed vigour. I still get goosebumps thinking about it.

So now, on 12 May 2021, I am on my way again to the heights of Cebreiro in the same place on the Camino Francès. Thanks to the corona pandemic, the route is an oasis of peace. It is May in 'hot Spain', but last night it was freezing. It is snowing and storming. The wind whistles around my ears and a kilo of mud hangs from each shoe.

That dear old man in Peshawar comes back to my mind now.

In that chaotic bustle, I did not realise at the time that this would be a turning point for me. Those few sentences, and especially the feeling they released, never left me again. They have been the start of a quest beyond the scientist I had mainly been until then. And if I had looked and listened better around me, I could have seen that my wife had been on that same quest for a long time, but I didn't understand it then.

> Meanwhile, I read a similar experience in **Carl Jung's autobiography** in conversation with the chief of the Pueblo Indians:
> 'I was amazed to see how the Indian's facial expression changes as soon as he talks about his religious ideas. In everyday life, he shows considerable self-control and dignity. On the other hand, when he talks about things that touch his mysteries, he is seized by a surprising emotion that he can't hide. He said, pointing to the sun: Is he who goes there not our father? How can you say anything else? How can there be another God? Nothing can exist without the sun. I (Carl Jung) asked him if he did not think that the sun is a fiery ball formed by an invisible God. My question did not even arouse surprise, let alone reluctance. He didn't even think my question was stupid. It left him completely cold. The only answer I got was: The sun is God. Everyone can see that. '

Later, I came to understand that the man from Peshawar and also the Indian have an inner certainty. They don't want to convince anyone.

Looking back, I see very clearly how frequent deep contact with people outside our own European culture has changed me. Deep contact is sometimes easier with strangers than with acquaintances.

Although I have remained a scientist.

Over the years, a total vision has emerged. That vision is not finished. It is in constant motion, evolution.

I have always resisted the urge to write everything down. Other people are smarter than me and making something tangible like sculpture is more my thing. I hate computers... But here, on the Camino, on the road to Cebreiro, I feel I have to do this. I start jotting down random ideas as I walk. I'll elaborate on it later. So this book will always be connected to the spiritual route of the Camino.

It is the report of a spiritual journey within myself. A quest to connect modern science, humanism and the major world religions. I will try to show that they share the same qualities and deficiencies. Science and humanism also have all the characteristics of a religion. I will come back to that later. Not to destroy something, but to bring a story of connection: they essentially mean the same thing, only the details are different: 'God and man are equal...' (at least if you take the theory of relativity and quantum mechanics among the natural sciences). I think of Simone Weil: 'Every religion has a core of truth in which love of fellow human beings and goodness is central'. This is also true for sciences, although the technological execution of new inventions often falls far short here.

Religion, humanism and science are essentially deep and honest searches for truth.

> **Niels Bohr, founder of quantum mechanics:** 'The opposite of a correct observation is a wrong observation. But the opposite of a profound truth may well be another profound truth. '

The face of the old man in Peshawar slides before my gaze again and I think of another quote by Simone Weil: 'The absolute goodness of God reveals itself in the face of the other'.

2. Objective observation and reasoning are the basis of the natural sciences

August 6, 2006, Pechawar, Pakistan (see photo 1 on www.scienceandspirituality.be, qr-code p7)

We take a motor rickshaw to the old city centre. It's impressive. A man shows us around in a beautiful mosque with caravanserai, where we talk to students. He tells us about the ancient Silk Road, and takes us into some small alleys. Another man tells us how he builds musical instruments... In a bazaar like this, you keep coming across real craftsmanship. It's nice how people tell this with love, even though they know you don't need a bicycle or a musical instrument.

Until... we end up in a mosque where only I am allowed in. I am harassed by a student who asks me:

- Do you notice the difference here between people who strictly observe the Quran like us, and the others?

- No, I wouldn't know, but I do notice a lot of difference in the treatment of men and women: my wife is not allowed in here!

- That's so not to distract the man.

- Why? Allah didn't create women?

- Yes, she may be there, but she must not arouse desire, which is why she must be veiled.

- Why? Surely Allah also created sexuality? Didn't he do

well then? Was man perhaps better made differently? Then couldn't he have created it that way? Or change it? Can't he do everything?

End of conversation. I detect great doubt in the student's eyes.

A second student is more persistent. I reproduce a small part of the long conversation:

- You are rich, but not happy. You have no peace in your heart.

- For you, I am rich, but not in Belgium. I have peace in my heart because I was able to follow my vocation. This is being a teacher and a father.

- You only live for a short time. 60 or 70 years. What do you do then, when you come before Allah?

- Or maybe tomorrow, who knows...? I'm not lying awake at night because of that. We'll see then. It's now that counts!

- Then you will weep, think of me and regret that you didn't convert to Islam!

- I don't believe it. Science can show that many ideas of the Bible and the Koran are outdated.

- Just as a mother prefers to see her own children, Allah prefers to see a Muslim.

- Why does Allah send earthquakes here, and not at our place?

- There are not enough real Muslims.

- Then Allah is not righteous because your kind of religion just depends on your place of birth....

The conversation goes on for quite some time, and I think once more how important it is in educating to form people who really think. You can open the mind through science or literature so that you don't just find everything is 'normal'.

I go outside and see Christine in a heated discussion with a group of men. One man thinks she does not even belong in the courtyard but this is too much for her:
'I'm walking here with a veil on my head, I'm not allowed to enter anywhere and it's not good still! What do you think?? I'm staying here whether you like it or not!!! I STAY!!!'

The biggest problem with beliefs and disinformation is the lack of curiosity for truth starting from observation.

Albert Einstein: 'I have no special talent. I am merely curious. '

February 26, 2019, Varanasi, India
I get into a conversation with a group of students on the banks of the Ganges while hearing the latest European Spanish-language summer hit from their smartphone. I hum along softly as I pass.
- Do you know this song?
- Yes, it's European, and that's where I live.
- Where exactly?
- In Belgium.
- Oh, there are good footballers there!
- What are you doing by the Ganges?

- We are studying at university here. We would love to come to Europe or America to study, though. Most of all, we would love to live there for a while, taste that freedom, but our parents don't want us to. The West is too depraved...

- Oh yeah, what do you mean?

- Well, it seems (according to our parents) that a man can have sex with anyone there, but then he also doesn't know exactly who his children are. And that you are divorced in five minutes....

- Then you are not well informed after all. Just about everyone wants a stable, long-term relationship. Especially if you have children together. And you can indeed get divorced in my country. But that is always a very painful process, an emergency solution with a lot of sadness... But what's the point of staying together as two enemies? When it really doesn't work anymore?

- Yes, it is the truth but our parents are afraid of that. They want to marry us off. We don't want that anymore. Still, sometimes I find it decadent in your place! Recently I saw on television that Europeans have two taps in the kitchen: one for water and one for beer!

- I don't know anyone who has this.

- Yes, we noticed a whole pipe network with beer, underground!

- Oh but now I understand! This is about the production of 'Brugse Zot'. To be a Bruges beer, it has to be produced in

You have to look critically for what is objectively true and try to eliminate bias. Therefore, you also have to be open to opposing views. Religious people who contest natural science assume a perfectly ordered universe. They want to get rid of everything that doesn't fit their narrative. Take evolutionary theory, for example. This sweeping under the carpet of anything that doesn't fit what you take to be true is the biggest problem in analysing information for any of us, including scientists.

We can try to change this in ourselves by first distinguishing between 'proven, objective truths'. You can't ask questions about that. Another (big) part of science is hypothesis. In the sciences, sweeping under the carpet what doesn't fit deeply held hypotheses is as prevalent as in religions!

For example: The theory of evolution has been proven many times through fossils, by embryology and dating methods. So it is a false discussion to be for or against evolution. It is simply there. How humans evolved from Africa precisely is a hypothesis, so, not proven. And you can also doubt whether Darwin's theory is complete. Maybe we don't know all the factors that determine evolution? The latter in particular is super-sensitive in scientific circles. I'll come back to that in detail when I talk about the new information quantum mechanics gives us in relation to evolution.

In this context, a quote from **Etienne Vermeersch** (Belgian philosopher):

'God cannot be infinitely powerful and infinitely good and merciful at the same time, otherwise the world would be a bit nicer. '

This is correct. You cannot doubt this, because if God were omnipotent, He could instantly make man's nature a little more peaceful. Either He is not infinitely merciful, and thinks the misery on earth is good. Either He is merciful, but cannot change man. Then God is not omnipotent. From this 'correct' reasoning, Vermeersch concludes that there can be no God. This has also been my decision for many years.

Carl Jung, as a scientist, gives a completely different answer: 'Our conception of god, our image of god, is not correct. But I have become certain in the course of my life that the Divine exists. '

So truth really does exist, although objective observation and reasoning are extremely difficult. For everyone. Even in science. Because we are biased or perceive incorrectly. Take our image of the earth. Surely we 'see' that the sun revolves around the earth? We 'see' that the earth is flat, don't we?

But we are not looking precisely! On a clear day, you can 'see' very clearly that the belly of a 'far' container ship is below the horizon if you stand on the North Sea beach. The curvature of the earth lies in front of it. On top of a dune, you can then see that ship completely because you look out above the curvature.

In 300 BC, **Aristotle** already suspected that the earth was spherical because travellers travelling south see the southern constellations higher above the horizon. Because stars are very far away, which he suspected even then, this is only possible if the horizon in more southern regions makes an angle with the horizon in more northern regions, i.e. if the surface of the earth is curved. So the surface of the earth is not flat!

An even easier observation is that during the partial phase of a lunar eclipse the shadow edge of the earth on the moon is always round, regardless of how high the moon is above the horizon. Only a sphere casts a round shadow in any direction, while a round, flat disk casts an elliptical shadow in most directions.

Despite these observations, doubts remained due to the bias of the Biblical worldview. Until September 1522: the only remaining boat of F. Magellan's expedition docked in Spain after a full voyage around the world... It was proven.

So in this book, I will try to 'see objectively', starting from science. What is the purpose of this world, of our lives? What is the future of the earth?

In particular, evolutionary theory forms the starting point. And for a special reason: if we understand our past and get to know the laws of evolution open-mindedly, we can try to apply those laws to our evolution in the future .

> **Golo Mann (historian***):*** 'He who does not know his past will not get a grip on the future. '

And we are privileged observers! Relativity theory and quantum mechanics have opened up new perspectives in recent years.

3. But 'seeing objectively' is not enough

Personally I'm very moved by the work of **Pierre Teilhard de Chardin** , where he explained his revolutionary vision of evolution in 'The phenomenon of man' in the 1930s and how religion and science flow here together. For me this is a masterpiece.

In this context, another excerpt from the conversation between Carl Jung and the Puebla chief:

> *'Look'*, said **Ochwia Biano**: *'The whites always want something, they are always restless and agitated. We don't know what they want. We don't understand them. We believe they are crazy'.* I (**Carl Jung**) asked him why then he thought white people were all crazy. He replied, *'They say they think with their heads'*. *'But of course. Where do you think then? '* I asked in surprise. *'We think here'* he said and pointed to his heart. '

And admit it. What would we be without intuition, imagination, music, art*?*

> **Albert Einstein**: 'Imagination is more important than knowledge. There are only two ways to live your life: pretending that nothing is a miracle and pretending that everything is a miracle. I believe in the latter way. '

Intuition and imagination drive scientific research forward. You can't do without that 'flash'! Even in science.

All the great scientists were very intuitive. Most of them deeply religious. Newton had pondered the question for years: Why do apples fall? Under that apple tree, he had a sudden inspiration, a 'flash', which led to the wonderful formula of gravity. That formula, amazing in its simplicity, was a revolution and one of the pillars of classical mechanics.

Poincaré had earlier arrived at the same calculations as Einstein. However, he did not recognise the new picture of space and time that his equations showed him. Thanks to Einstein's great intuition as a physicist, the step to the theory of relativity was possible.

And there is another strange thing going on with intuition. Many important inventions are linked to a name, but if that or that scientist did not develop the theory, another did at the same time. Take the theory of evolution again, for instance. Darwin elaborated and wrote it down, but the idea was not new. He was building on ideas that were growing, fermenting. Should he not have published his book, others would surely have done so in his place....

Intuition is thus precisely in touch with 'something in common'. The 'collective unconscious'*(glossary at the back) is certainly a part of this. According to Jung, this is a kind of repository of latent images that humans as a species have inherited from their past, a past that includes both animal and human ancestors.
Synchronicity is also extremely important in the development of all new ideas. Synchronicity means that several events seem to

be connected, creating a positive or surprising outcome. There is no causal link between those events; it seems like coincidence.

You cannot command intuition. It happens to you, or, if you want something, it just doesn't happen.

When creating an artwork, this can be extremely difficult. Many years ago, I had a good friend with whom I did some camping treks in the mountains. We lost touch for 20 years. Until I happened to hear that his son had died. Because of that, I contacted him again, and thus received a funeral card of the boy.

The penetrating photos of the card immediately made me feel the urge to paint a portrait of the boy. That didn't go smoothly. I couldn't get a connection with it. At the same time, I was also working on a sculpture in ceramic: 'the circle of life', a mother and child expressing their connection to life in a circular form. It had nothing to do with that. That too didn't want to go smoothly...
With a big sigh and rather displeased, I move away from my modelling table and painting easel... I walk down the stairs and suddenly get this flash: you don't have to make that painting, but the statue is for them! I return, on a whim, cut the child free from the circle and place it on the mother's lap. The connection was made. Then I was able to finish the sculpture in a few days, and the painting, too....
Two events seemingly unrelated... Synchronicity.

Conclusion: This book is scientifically structured. We try to 'see', 'observe', analyse, reason. Here you are not permitted doubt. But that's not enough. You have to build further on intuition. This is extremely important, also in the science. I will clearly indicate the distinction between the two.

> **Albert Einstein**: 'Intuition' is a godsend. And reasoning a servant. Somewhere along the way we started worshipping the servant and forgot the gift. '

Chapter 2

The amazing story of the great world religions

Pierre Teilhard de Chardin (1933)

'In the next century, all the major world religions will be in trouble, yet the next century will be the century of the religious man. '

November 29, 2012: Jerusalem, Israel

It is 5am and still dark. I am on the Via Dolorosa, the agony road of Christ. It is still very early in the morning. The road is deserted, the souvenir shops are closed. I focus on the various 'stations' of the Way of the Cross and let the ancient route work on me. A sense of connection with all the suffering of humanity, with all that is, overwhelms me. For the last five stations, you enter the Church of the Holy Sepulchre. Impressive when the silence shimmers, like so many places in the city. You feel connected to the unspeakable.

After the complete 'Stations of the Cross', I become more aware of my surroundings again. My stomach growls, it is time for breakfast. So I stroll again down the Via Dolorosa , also the artery of the Arab trading district.

- Salam aleikum (Peace be upon you). Can I have breakfast with coffee here?

- Of course! Wa alaikum assalam wa rahmutullah (Peace be upon you and so be the mercy and blessings of Allah.)

The shops open their doors one by one: vegetables, fruit, kebabs, souvenirs... An unimaginable bustle erupts. I myself am still deeply impressed what I just experienced....

Suddenly, a totally different bustle. A crowd of people in brown penitent clothes with white rope around their waists, barefoot, stream into the alley. Whips for self-flagellation would be in place here. Candles illuminate the group and there are loud prayers, chants. The whole road becomes one brown tide. I have to move quickly to clear the road completely. The Arab man who brought my breakfast looks a little scared and takes a deep breath as the group has passed. You notice that getting in the way of these people would lead to trouble very quickly. With myself, the sense of connection is now completely broken off.

Historically, it is easy to trace how the Via Dolorosa arose in the course of history. This is not the road Christ took to Golgotha. It is also very unlikely that the Church of the Holy Sepulchre is in the right place. But that doesn't mean it's only a story. The connection to the 'collective unconscious' is enormous. And this is as real and valuable as if it would be historically accurate. It's not surprising Muslims, Christians and Jews regard Jerusalem as a holy city.

But that is precisely the problem with many religions: clinging to the 'literal interpretation' of their texts against their better judgement. And it can also be worse: wanting others to behave accordingly. This is how aggressiveness arises.

Israel is a country where all those contradictions are at their sharpest. It is a fascinating country and I reflect on it for a while because it is the basis for 3 major faith communities on our planet. It is the most religious country in the world, though the Western countries don't realise that. In no other country in the world does public life come to a complete standstill on the Sabbath. Against the will of most people, even there. There is no public transport on Saturdays. In Jerusalem, cinemas are banned. And even the Arab population (this is 21%, not counting East Jerusalem and the occupied territories, otherwise a lot more) has to obey those laws as well.

You can never get the coexistence of peoples resolved that way. Let us look objectively at the Jewish story. Claiming the territory of Israel rests on the historical basis of the Bible and the Diaspora* (= the violent dispersal of the entire Jewish people by the Romans in 37 AD). You can demonstrate via scientific research that neither is correct.

What historical ground does the Bible have? Bible science can easily prove that Abraham and all the other patriarchs were not real persons. The story of 'killing Isaac' (Genesis 22, 1-13) appears as myth in other religions. Moses too is a mythical figure: we find the story of the basket on the Nile (Exodus 2, 1 - 10)) in a number of myths, spread all over the world. I'll come back to this later.

It may be historically correct that there were several waves of immigration from Egypt to Canaan (present-day Israel) around 2000 B.C. Immigration would have started before the time of Moses. Also very unlikely is that a journey of barely 500 km took 40 years. No archaeological remains from that period have been found in the Sinai desert either. 40 years is a symbolic number in many religions, including in the New Testament where Jesus spends 40 days in the desert. And... for those who remember, our 'fast' and the 'ramadan' also lasts 40 days.

After crossing the Sinai desert, the Jews arrived in Canaan (present-day Israel) The Jews' conquest of existing cities - such as Jerusalem - was certainly not a massacre. On the contrary, the city remained Canaanite and many of the cultic customs that had been established were adopted. Various groups of Jews gradually trickled in, one of which may have been led by a certain Moses. The Jews were not a homogeneous group. Many married Canaanite women and assimilated in that time. In **Luke Catherine**'s book 'The Layered Religion', you can easily follow well the Old Testament story emerged later as a myth, a conglomeration of two or more cultures.

The Jewish diaspora* is also only partly true. DNA research of the Jewish people has proven several times that this story is wrong. It is also visible. How can Jewish communities in Europe look so European? Indian communities look very Indian, and the 'Ethiopian tribe' then typical Ethiopian. However, most Jews do have slightly more genes related to the region called 'the Levant' (this is the broad surroundings of Israel) than people in Eastern Europe, India or Ethiopia. Yet, it has been shown several times that most Jews are converts, and Palestinians actually have the most 'originally Jewish genes'....Those converts formed separate communities, who were often treated unfairly because of their 'being different'.

The Christian religion is also not a story to be taken literally. If you take it literally, the various gospels in the New Testament contradict each other. The Q gospel, according to scholarly Bible study, is said to be at the basis of all the gospels. This book, in turn, has clear links to the oldest religion in India: Hinduism. When Christianity came to Europe via the Romans, it was mixed with many Celtic and Germanic elements. The Celtic elements in particular also have ties with India, Egypt, etc.

Studying those connections is particularly fascinating to find the objective truth behind many disagreements. You can also see the interconnectedness of total humanity appearing in such studies. And I also want to make it very clear at once here that I'm not in any way diminishing the value of the Jewish or Christian tradition. On the contrary!

10 October 2019, Mashad (Iran)

After a night on the Tehran - Mashad sleeper train, I'm arriving at one of the entrances of the second largest shrine in the world of Shiite Muslims:

- Halt! Oh dear. I get stopped and have to wait for a 'mandatory guide'

After a while, a member of the Revolutionary Guard appears to 'accompany' me.

- I am Mohammed, a member of the Revolutionary Guard.

- My name is Johan, I want to come and pray at the grave of Imam Resa.

- You cannot do this as an non-believer. I will guide you as you visit the various mosques.

- I am not a non-believer.

- Are you a Muslim then?

- No, I do not have a particular kind of faith, yet I am deeply religious.

- How then?

- I am a scientist by education, but I know very well that there is more, that all people are connected.

- Yes, but you either believe that man was created by God or came into existence through evolution.

- I don't think this is a contradiction, not accepting the theory of evolution is being wilfully blind, because it has been proven many, many times. But to assume that only random changes in genetic material (mutations) drive evolution is a choice of 'materialistic science'. To me, everything has a purpose. Evolution is a beautiful system. I

cannot do otherwise than see more behind it, as do almost all great scientists.

We talk for hours and patiently listen to each other's opinions. Mohammed understands that evolution is correct but can easily integrate that into his faith. I have great respect for him. For the way he listens, the way he is committed to his country. In a few hours, a deep friendship was born here. I get a one-week entrance permit, but still he advises me to go to Iman Resa's grave only when I'm done internally.

I stay in Mashad for 4 days and go back to the shrine many times. At any time of the day, sometimes even in the middle of the night. I am completely overwhelmed by the energy that is present here and completely unexpectedly, while sitting on the bus to the mountains, I have a beautiful spiritual experience. Because I take the time to be really present here, this can happen.

Through scientific study, we can clear up misunderstandings, we can bridge differences...

But, we can never fully understand the world. I will demonstrate this further when discussing relativity theory and quantum mechanics. We need images, myths for that. Religions and also science are full of them. Think of the 'primeval mother Mary'. These same powerful themes tend to recur in art. Michelangelo's Pieta...

Art, mysticism, gives access to the world where it really matters. We can't live without it. Many images and myths are universal and take a different form depending on religion or culture. Most primal stories are found everywhere. Think of the deluge, this even appears with native Americans.... They have been passed on to each other throughout human history, all the way with man's journey through the Bering Strait to the Americas...! We are all related to each other. Which images are 'appropriate' for you to imagine the universe is less important.

Or you can actually conclude: All religions and myths are historically mostly inaccurate, but still real if they are real to you. For me, the Via Dolorosa is 'real' but historically inaccurate. The image of the Indian chief is 'real' but scientifically incorrect because the sun is a fireball and will one day cease to exist.

> **Niels Bohr** (founder of quantum mechanics): 'Personally, I find the division of the world into an objective and a subjective side far too arbitrary. The fact that religions over the centuries have spoken in images, parables and paradoxes simply means that there are no other ways of knowing the reality they refer to. But that does not mean this is not a real. And dividing the reality into an objective and a subjective side will not get us very far.'

I want to dwell on humanism for a moment here. For me, a true humanist is not an unbeliever, but a deeply religious person: love for human beings and daring to question one's own ideas and those of others. Art, literature, nature and mankind are a source of inspiration. Belief in the power of humanity and respect for it as a special part of nature are central.

I hope we can leave behind the apparent contradictions, allow each other the freedom to use the religion, the culture, the images, that suit us and focus on what unites us. It will really be needed in tomorrow's world.

Where did we come from and where are we going? What scientific laws can we deduce to look to our future?

Chapter 3

The natural sciences show us a wonderful predictable world

> **Thomas Aquinas**: 'The greatest pleasure consists in beholding the truth. But every pleasure relieves pain. And therefore the beholding of truth reduces sadness and pain. The more perfectly a person loves wisdom, the more pain can be released.'

Modern science has changed our static, biblical worldview into a dynamic system. Everything is constantly changing: living species change, continents move, the universe does not stay the same...We are also no longer at the centre of our view of the world. We are a puny species on a tiny planet, well engaged in destroying ourselves, created by chance, without a single reason for existence.

Tremendous progress has been made thanks to specialization in many different disciplines of science. But the sense of totality has been lost. Hardly anyone sees the whole anymore. Moreover, science has increasingly come to behave like a religion. And religions have two negative characteristics in addition to the many positive ones: they do not tolerate contradiction and can explain everything with 'god'. The god of science is chance. What we don't understand is coincidence. But admit it. How could that beautiful world and that grand universe ever have come into being by blind chance? Fortunately, mechanisms have been found in quantum mechanics that more than direct this 'coincidence', and this fascinating branch of science is only in its infancy.

> **Robbert Oppenheimer 1949:** 'There should be no limits to freedom of research. There is no place for dogmas in science. The scientist is free and, in order correcting errors, must be free to ask any question and seek any evidence.'

For now, the universe we live in is a four-dimensional entity. Three space dimensions (length, width, height) and time. Because of the time dimension, the universe is not purposeless but an evolving system. And there is also unity: everything influences everything.

To understand the evolving universe, it is indispensable to study Darwin's theory of evolution. The unity and character of this universe can only be understood if some basic principles of the theory of relativity and quantum mechanics are also discussed. And to understand those basic principles, it is indispensable to see through the structure of the universe and matter.

1. The unimaginable largeness of the universe

25 January 2007, Darwin- Alice Springs, Australia

The bus ride, right through the 'outback' (inland) is beautiful. One of the most inhospitable areas in the world. The road cuts through an area sparsely forested. Grasses are budding in abundance now because it is rainy season. The dark red earth and the heat bring us in a strange daze, we drive into the soul of Australia. A very different Australia. It teems with Aborigines at every stop. Whites are a minority here. Many Aborigines are in bad shape! They are vagabonds. They hang around, unkempt. Some are drunk. A man comes up to us and says: 'diseases, alcoholism and unemployment are common among the original people of this continent'. These people are completely displaced. It is a sad sight. However, before the arrival of Europeans, this people had the wisdom to live in harmony with nature in one of the world's most extreme places...

Today we drive 'under the sun'. On 21/12, the sun was right above the Tropic of Capricorn, which is at 23° south latitude, or just the location of Alice Springs. The sun is now slowly moving up (seemingly), towards the equator, where it will be right above on 21/3. So you can easily calculate that the sun is vertically above the latitude line of 14° south latitude today. This is just south of Katherin. We stop there precisely at 12.30 p.m. I take a picture of a vertical pole in the sun, with no shadow next to it. Stunning! For the first time in my life, I'm standing right under the sun and I'm moved. Until now, the sun was in the south at midday. From now on, it will be in the north! And you notice it very well because we are driving straight south. After half an hour, you see that the road signs give a little shadow again, but now to the south. It is a wonderful experience to be able to see this with your own eyes!

It was already known in ancient times that if you travelled far enough south along the Nile, there was a moment in the year when there was no more shadow. The astronomers' explanation of this phenomenon at the time was unfortunately lost in the great fire of the library of Alexandria. We had to wait thousands more years for Galileo, and especially Kepler's laws, to fully understand the internal movement of our solar system....

There is further enjoyment. The vegetation becomes scarcer. The sun slowly sinks below the horizon, setting the landscape to the west in a fiery red glow... The first stars... The landscape moves further under the twinkling stars.

The universe is about 13.7 billion years old. We can't observe 72% of it in any way. That's why we call it 'dark energy'. We know that this energy exists by studying the movement of the stars in the universe.

Of the remaining 28%, 24% is 'dark matter', also not observable to us in any way. The remaining 4% are elementary particles (protons, neutrons and electrons, see further). Three-fourths of these are invisible. So when we talk about the observable universe, we are talking about 4% of the universe! About the rest, we know little or nothing.

So we must remain humble. Yet what we have come to know about that 4% over the last few centuries is not futile. In fact, it is fantastic!

We live on the beautiful blue planet Earth. One moon revolves around our planet in 28 days. (A moon is a celestial body that revolves around a planet.) In turn, our earth revolves around the sun in 365.26 days. Because of the Earth's tilted axis, we get differences per season. The further from the equator, the greater the differences between the seasons.

But, we do not revolve alone around the sun. There are eight of us: Mercury, Venus, Earth, Mars, Jupiter, Saturn, Uranus and Neptune. And also five dwarf planets (including Pluto) and more than a million known asteroids. 644 moons orbit around planets and asteroids. And also the 3701 known comets... (status: January 2021) This seems like a lot, but the space around the sun is huge.

If in your imagination the sun is an orange on the table before you, the earth is 1200 km away! (Search for a place on the map, 1200 km away from the place you live) We can then imagine that 'earth so far away' as a pinhead....

But you will also find some other larger or smaller pinheads in a much larger space: the other planets. A pinhead and an orange in a 1200 km space sphere take up almost no space. Yet the orange (the sun) is 99.86% of the mass in our solar system. Not surprisingly, all those 'pinheads' orbit around the sun. That sun is one giant nuclear power plant, an immense fireball...

The whole of our sun with its planets and their moons is called the solar system.

But the solar system is not alone. When you see the starry sky, it's hard to imagine that every little star is actually the same nuclear power station as our sun. With planets and moons around it over and over. Take the Pole Star, for example. Like the sun forms the solar system, the Pole Star forms the 'Pole Star System'.

Around 100 billion stars shine in our 'environment'. Each with their planets. Together in the universe, they form a giant flat disc: the Milky Way. Our solar system lies somewhat on the edge of that disc.

Imagine a flat, giant dinner plate compressed by grains of sand. Our solar system is a grain of sand on the edge of the plate. If we look from that grain of sand towards the outside of the plate, we see only a few more grains of sand: the separate stars in the sky. If we look towards the inside of the plate, we see a mass of sand grains: the two luminous bands of the Milky Way. The board slowly rotates around its centre...

The stars in that giant flat disc (the Milky Way) revolve around their center in 220 million years: a giant black hole.

But the Milky Way is not alone! There are 2,000 billion other star groups! All consisting of billions of stars, with their planets, moons... We call such a group of stars a galaxy.

All those galaxies are flying away from each other at a gigantic speed. This is the expansion of the universe.

And then those distances. We already cannot realize the distances within our own 'small' solar system....
To represent the enormous distances in the universe, we use the term light second, light minute, light year, etc. As follows: Light travels 300,000 km per second. So two light seconds mean 600,000 km. The distance sun - earth is about 150,000,000 km. The distance is therefore 500 light-seconds or 8.3 minutes. So if we look at the sun, this is an image that is actually 8.3 minutes old. If the sun were to extinguish, we could actually see this only 8.3 minutes later. The nearest star (Proxima Centauri) is 4.2 light years away. So we see that star as it looked 4.2 years ago.

> But that doesn't mean we can fly at that speed! Voyager I left Earth in 1977 and has now crossed the boundaries of our solar system. It is still racing and is the farthest spaceship to ever leave Earth. Yet it is only 22 light hours away from Earth. With that enormous speed, it would reach our nearest star (Proxima Centauri) within 17,000 years...

The Andromeda Nebula (the closest other galaxy in our neighbourhood) is 2,537,000 light years away. So when we peer through the Hubble telescope, we see the Andromeda Nebula as it looked 2.5 million years ago! This is beyond our imagination...

Despite the immensity of space and matter, you notice that this is not a disorderly system. In fact, there is an enormous unity because the entire universe is composed of the same matter according to an ordered system. Galaxies all revolve around their axis, planets revolve around the stars, moons around the planets... and so on. And yet no endless repetition: every planet, every star, every moon is different: in the system there is endless creativity...!

When you let this sink in, you are overwhelmed... And this is only about 4% of the universe...!

2. The unimaginable smallness of the atom

How is everything you see around you constructed?

Over the course of the last century, we have been able to walk on the moon, explore Mars and look into the sweltering deserts of Venus. We took pictures of all the planets of our solar system. We discovered planets around other stars (exoplanets). Even one in another galaxy! But actually, we mainly examined rock. Stones from space are of course fascinating, but for most non-geologists there is not much difference between a 'moon rock' and a 'Mars rock' . The basic composition is always the same.

However, there is one place in our solar system where the basic ingredients of rocks and stones have such a variety of shapes and functions that just one gram of the material shows more variation than all the matter studied from space. That place, of course, is the little blue planet, our Earth. So for now, it may be enough to study matter here to understand the rest of our solar system...

The things you see around you are usually not pure substances. Earth, water, air... etc. are mixtures of several substances. For example, air consists of a mixture of nitrogen, oxygen, carbon dioxide, and a number of other gases. Or seawater consists of water and salt, among other things. You can separate the substances in a mixture. For example, if you let seawater evaporate, salt is a residue. If you collect the water vapour from warm seawater and cool it again, you get pure water (this is how drinking water is made in many Arabian desert countries). Salt and water are pure substances. There are no other substances mixed into them. Or we can say that mixtures consist of *pure substances*.

You can further divide an amount of pure substance: For example, a litre of water can be divided into two. Then you have two half-litres. Again in two. Then you have 250 ml. Again in two, again and again...etc . You now have one drop of water. You divide that drop further into two and then again into two, then again and again, etc... At a certain moment you have the smallest particle of water. We call this smallest particle that still has all the properties of water a **molecule**. One molecule is still water, is still salt. If you now divide a molecule further, you no longer have water, salt... but the *parts* that make up water or salt. We call those parts **atoms**. Atoms have completely different properties than the molecule where they are present. Atoms occur in a molecule in a specific amount.

> Imagine a city with many neighbourhoods. Each neighbourhood has a specific type of house. So I can divide the city (mixture) into districts with a certain type of house. (Pure substance) Now I can divide each neighbourhood into two, another into two...etc. At some point, I have the part of that neighbourhood that still has the habitation property, namely a house (molecule). If I divide further, I

get the building materials used to build that house (atoms). Those building materials have different properties than the house has. From the outside of the house, you wouldn't have thought there were big steel girder and water pipes. You cannot live in such a steel girder (=property). You can, however, build a bridge with it: the properties of the parts are different.

For example, if you split water (this is possible with electric current: electrolysis) into its parts, you get oxygen and hydrogen. Both are gaseous. Their properties have nothing to do with water anymore, although they are the components of water! You obtain twice as much hydrogen as oxygen with such electrolysis. Or: one molecule of water consists of 2 atoms of hydrogen and one atom of oxygen.

The construction materials of a house are needed in a certain quantity: 2 steel girders, 52 metres of water pipe,...

In summary: the basic components of any substance are its molecules. Molecules are made up of atoms that occur in a certain amount in the molecule.

So how are atoms constructed?

You can compare an atom to a tiny solar system. The sun is the nucleus of the atom: a small sphere in the centre of the atom. The 'planets' orbiting it are very much smaller spheres.

An atom is almost empty. 99.999...% of all mass is concentrated in the nucleus. Small particles spin around it: we call them *electrons*. They have a negative electrical charge.

> If you imagine the atom as a circle with a diameter of 30 km, the nucleus is a 30 cm football at the centre: a similar structure to the solar system!

Electrons can be detached from the atom. This is electricity.

> Our body is made also up of atoms. And even the atoms of our body are 99.999...% empty. If you were able to eliminate all that 'superfluous' empty space from atoms, matter would suddenly take up a lot less space. You could then compress the entire human race into a sugar cube...

Inside the nucleus you will find two types of building blocks: the protons (have a positive electrical charge) and the neutrons (no electrical charge). The nucleus of the atom is very stable. Yet you can split it. To do so, you need enormous forces. But once the fission, the splitting, gets going, you get a chain reaction. The amounts of energy then released are huge. We are in the domain of nuclear energy here. Think also of an atomic bomb where that energy is released at the same time!

Protons and neutrons consist of even smaller basic particles: the quarks. Most of the mass of the protons is not the mass of its parts (quarks) but of the energy of the empty space between the quarks. This is the turbulent 'brew' of particles that arise from 'nothingness' and then fall back into it. We often call this 'vibration'. (See later)

So our entire reality actually consists of only 3 basic particles: protons, neutrons and electrons! The universe, nature, the stars, the earth,... Incredible that only 3 tiny Lego bricks make up all this...!

In each atom the number of protons is equal to the number of electrons, making one atom electrically neutral. (= the number of positive charges of the protons is equal to the number of negative ones of the electrons)

The atoms differ because of their different number of protons. For example, you have a type of atom with one proton. We 'see' this as hydrogen. If the atoms have 2 protons, we see this as helium. 6 protons form carbon, 8 protons oxygen... etc. In this way we can theoretically continue up to 103. The larger this number, the heavier the atom, of course, because the protons and neutrons determine its mass. There are also a number of neutrons in each atom.

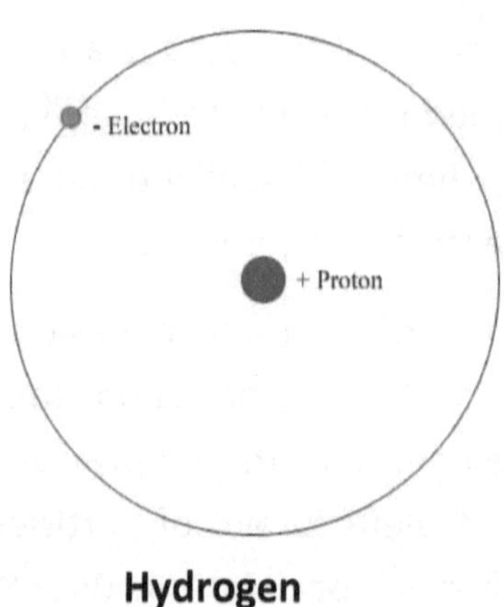

Hydrogen

For those wishing to delve a little further:

The electrons orbit around the nucleus in well-defined orbits or shells, just like in the universe. The difference is that there is more than one electron per orbit or shell (in the solar system, there is only one planet per orbit). The first shell has two places, the second 8, the third also 8. After that, larger shells follow for the heavier atoms: 18, 18, 32, 32.

Atoms strive for a full outer shell. Some atoms are built with a full shell. Think of helium. Since helium has 2 protons, it also has 2 electrons. So the first shell (two places!) is full. Helium has no need to supplement its outer shell with electrons from another atom, the shell is already naturally full: a 'noble gas'. Atoms with one or two electrons on the outer orbital or shell easily deliver them to another atom. Then their penultimate shell is full. Atoms that lack a few electrons on the outer shell easily take up a few electrons to fill their outer shell. This is how atoms complement each other and so you get a stable bond. For example: the one electron from each of the two hydrogen atoms is easily given up. Oxygen is short of two and wants to take them up. So oxygen wants to bond with two hydrogen atoms and gets 2 extra electrons to fill up its outer shell. So one oxygen and two hydrogen atoms complement each other perfectly, giving you a stable compound in this ratio: H_2O or water. Meaning: a molecule of water consists of 2 atoms of hydrogen (H) and one atom of oxygen (O) (see image below)

On the known table of Mendeljev, atoms are arranged under or next to each other according to those properties.

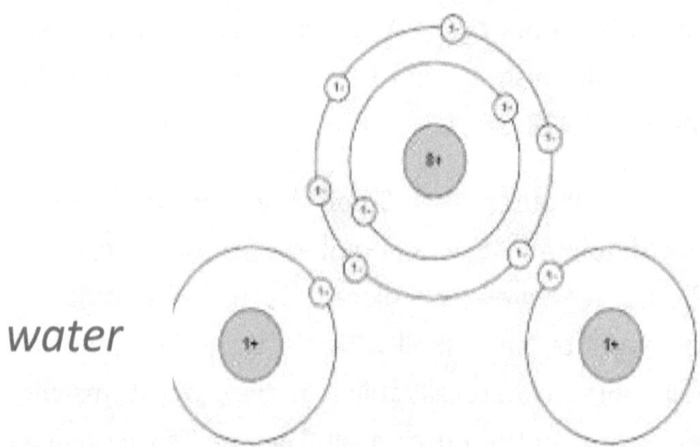

You see on the figure above one atom of oxygen the two smaller atoms of hydrogen, forming one water molecule.

Oxygen has 2 electrons short on the outer shell. One atom of carbon can give two atoms of oxygen a full shell with its 4 electrons. So those 4 electrons of carbon can be taken up by 2 oxygen atoms to form the stable compound CO_2: carbon dioxide. (see image below)

But carbon has another property. You notice in the drawing that the outer shell or orbit is just half-filled: 8 sites with 4 electrons and 4 open sites. Because carbon is just half-filled, it can also bond with itself and form long chains: in turns, a carbon atom takes in 4 electrons and the next one gives off 4 !

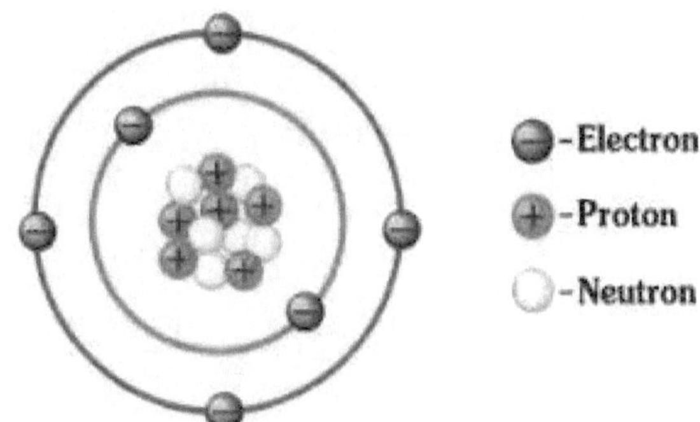

carbon: 4 electrons on the outer shell, and 4 open sites

This property of carbon is extremely important for the development of life. All living matter consists of carbon compounds. 'Fossil' fuels (wood, coal, petroleum, natural gas...) are compressed remains of former living things (plants, animals, micro-organisms...) and thus also consist mainly of carbon.

For some chemical reactions you need to add energy, from other reactions you get energy. For example, to split water into hydrogen and oxygen, you have to use electricity (= energy). If that electricity is produced with wind or solar energy, we call it 'green' hydrogen. The formation of water from hydrogen and oxygen is, of course, the reverse reaction and this is when energy is released. By the way, this is how a hydrogen engine works: you then use that energy to drive, and your car exhaust emission is only... water.

A second example: When making carbon dioxide (CO_2) from oxygen and carbon energy is released. Think of the heat energy released in a stove once the wood burns. Our entire industrial development is based on this process. Also the functioning of our bodies.

Briefly summarised:

Everything around you is made up of atoms. You can imagine any object (including your body) as a giant container of billions of very small marbles. One such marble is an atom. And each atom is a tiny solar system with a nucleus (the sun) where electrons (electrically negative particles) revolve. The nucleus consists of protons (electrically positive) and neutrons (uncharged). Like the solar system, the particles take up almost no space and the mass is almost entirely in the nucleus. So you can also represent the particles inside the atom by tiny balls or marbles. The largest marble is the nucleus; the much smaller marbles are the electrons circling around it.

Yet recent experiments show that the mass of the nucleus does not 'really' exist. The measured mass is mainly the energy between the moving parts of the protons (the quarks): we call this vibration.

Atoms differ from each other by the *number of* positive particles in the nucleus. For example, hydrogen has one. Carbon has six, oxygen 8, iron 26, gold 79, uranium 92... So we 'see' these substances as different because they have a different number of protons in the nucleus. Atoms can bond under certain conditions to form larger 'marbles' with different properties: the molecules. Normally, the same kind of atoms do not form larger molecules 'by themselves'. With carbon, this is different. Carbon atoms do bind to each other; they can form long chains.

So we see in matter an enormous unity: a few basic particles (protons, neutrons, electrons) form everything. But then again, there is that boundless creativity: the same basic particles keep forming other atoms, other molecules. Just like in the universe. The Andromeda Galaxy (our nearest neighbour) is completely different from the Milky Way. And on our own planet Earth creativity with atoms and molecules seems limitless....

Two big cracks in that beautiful predictable world...

It is as if we now fathom the nature of the world around us. But classical science is in fact a static view. The real engine of that immense creativity we explored has a deeper explanation. And its drive is so completely different! For the first time, we can use quantum mechanics and the theory of relativity to lift a small corner of the veil that lies on the engine of that immense creativity. We see a different world...

In all classical laws, mass and time are constant. A given mass is never lost. Even in chemistry. For example, if you let 1 kg of hydrogen and oxygen react with each other in the correct proportion, you will have 1kg of water, or 1 litre. The atoms are simply rearranged into another molecule. This is also true when you form CO_2, for example.

But **Albert Einstein** showed that this is only true in terrestrial conditions in classical chemistry. In nuclear energy and in the universe, it is a very different story...

And then time. Time seems to have a constant progression (our watches run the same, don't they?) but that is not true either. Time does not run the same everywhere in the universe! This is beyond comprehension.

And... It's not enough yet! Quantum mechanics turns the world really upside down...

None of us has integrated the 'new science' into our thinking because our mind works with constant time, a three-dimensional space around us and atoms or electrons that can be measured. So we ourselves think like classical science!!!

And the more we 'think' (as in our Western societies) the harder it is to accept this new reality. I myself could only do so when the evidence for some quantum mechanical phenomena was really proved with experiments. Only then I could accept that bizarre theory. Einstein never accepted it because there was no evidence then. But after his death he was proved wrong... Even among most scientists, the classical or materialistic view is still dominant.

You can almost put next to each other many of the new insights with the stories from many religions... Religions are telling in myths and stories a deeper, incomprehensible reality.

> **Niels Bohr (founder of quantum mechanics***):*** 'Whoever claims to understand quantum mechanics has understood nothing of it...'

We will now trying to look at the implications of these two fantastic theories that have been demonstrated by many experiments. An even more wonderful world will open up for you! (chapters 4, 5 and 6) And in chapters 7 to 12, we can look at their influence on our own history (our evolution) and try to deduce the laws (the 6 laws of evolution). Through those laws that determined the past, we can also look at our future (chapters 13, 14 and 15: the future of the Earth)

May I invite you tonight, or at any other time in a dark place, to admire the stars? Lie in a warm sleeping bag. Maybe you will recognise the Great Bear and the Pole Star or the Orion constellation with its reaching longbow? Or maybe not. If you are in a dark place, you can admire the double light strip of the Milky Way. Now think about what you have read and be overwhelmed by the majesty of it all. Read the previous part many times and watch, not just until you understand, but until you have absorbed it all and feel how you become a part of this mystery. Then look at your hands. They are made up of carbon atoms. Every atom of the billions of atoms that make up your hands are as superb as our solar system and all the stars you see around you. Keep your eyes open and flirt with sleep. You float at the edge of that mysterious cave and become one. Whole with the universe....Let it sink in. Mental knowledge is only a little part. Let it engulf you...Until you feel everything under your chest.... Then you are ready for the next: 'modern science'.

Chapter 4

The mystery of the theory of relativity

1. The fabulous link between mass and energy

Albert Einstein's formula **E = mc²** says that energy (E) is equal to mass (m) multiplied by the speed of light (c) squared. That speed of light is always 300,000 km/s. There can never be a higher speed. In short, it means that energy and mass can swap places. Energy can be stored in substances with mass, and that energy can be released later.

So what does the speed of light have to do with mass and energy? Imagine a space shuttle going almost as fast as light. The pilot keeps adding energy to the engines, but that energy cannot be used to exceed the speed of light. (maximum 300,000 km/s) On the other hand, that energy cannot disappear either. The first thermodynamic law says that energy can change form, but the 'amount of energy' always remains. So it is compressed into mass. The space shuttle becomes heavier. E (energy) becomes m (mass).

The sun is a reverse example. Every second, tonnes of hydrogen (mass) disappear and are converted into helium and energy.

Here's how it happens: the sun's fuel is hydrogen. A hydrogen atom has one proton in the atomic nucleus, which is why it is hydrogen. When two nuclei of hydrogen atoms collide, an atom of helium (He) is formed. This releases a huge amount of energy. The helium atom weighs less than the two atoms of hydrogen together, or mass is converted into energy. In a hydrogen bomb, unfortunately, this also happens. A hydrogen bomb is an uncontrolled reaction, but if we could control this process (nuclear fusion), we would have a nuclear power plant without dangerous waste materials. Great advances have been made in fusion technology, but before 2050 the technology will not be ready.

Also, in any nuclear power plant where atomic nuclei of heavier atoms (e.g. uranium has 92 protons) are split, mass is converted to energy. This is how our current nuclear power plants work.

So, all matter on earth is 'condensed' energy. And if that energy could be released, a sheet of paper could already be enough for the country's entire energy supply. But it's not easy to release that energy for the time being. The fuels we use to get energy (like petrol) only release a fraction of the energy stored in that matter.

2. A persistent illusion about time

Time is not a constant, linear event: at high speed, time slows down. We call this *time dilation or 'stretching'*. There is no such thing as one singular time, except in our mind...

April 2007, Wadi Halfa, Sudan (see photo 2 on www.scienceandspirituality.be)
Yesterday we reserved our seat on the bus in the normal way, but we don't exactly know what time the bus leaves. The owner says at 2pm. The police at 4pm and the people at 5pm. We might best believe the owner. At 2pm, the engine is already running. The musical horn blares waking up the whole village: *'quick, quick, we have to leave immediately!* 'Phew', good thing we were on time. The 'bus' is an open steel vehicle whose seats are twice too narrow even for anorexia patients. The colossus shoots away, as if it were for the final of the international bus races. But what happens? The songs keep going around Wadi Halfa until the bus is packed. It becomes 3 pm, 4 pm, 5 pm... Or everyone is right: the bus does indeed leave at 2 pm, but also at 3 pm, 4 pm... Well what is time here?
The only reason we can all synchronise our clocks is because we live on the same planet with the same gravity and revolve around the same sun at the same speed in the rotation system of the same Galaxy. So we all experience more or less the same sense of time because we are (almost) stationary opposite each

other. But in space, this is no longer true. Time depends on speed and gravity. And this differs everywhere in the universe.

In 1971, researchers at the U. S. Naval Observatory conducted an experiment to test time dilation . They made flights around the world in both directions, each circuit taking about three days. The planes carried four super-accurate atomic clocks . When they returned and compared their clocks with the Observatory clock in Washington, D. C., they had gained about 0.15 microseconds compared to the ground clock. The pilots had aged 0.15 microseconds less than those at the observatory! This matched Einstein's predictions.

Einstein on the death of his friend Besso: 'It means nothing that he left this strange world a little earlier than I. People like us who believe in physics know that the distinction between past, present and future is only a stubbornly maintained illusion.'

The earth rotates once every 24 hours. Earth's circumference (the equator) is 40,000 kilometres, so if you divide the distance by time (40,000/24), you get a rotation speed of 1,670 km per hour. But that's not all. The earth rotates around the sun at a speed of about 110,000 km/h. So we move super fast while sitting in our seats... But even that's not enough. The rotation of the Milky Way... And the expansion of the universe....
So sitting still is relative.

Relative time is often illustrated with twins where the one goes on (an imaginary) journey to a star light years away, while the other half remains on earth. The journey is almost as fast as light, and as we now know, time will pass more slowly for the travelling part of the twin than for the one standing still on earth. Because time moves slower for the astronaut than for the remaining half on Earth, the astronaut of the two will also age slower. When he returns home, he will be a few years younger than his twin brother.

An object has spatial properties: length, width and height (= 3 dimensions) Einstein adds another property to describe that object: time. Just as you could add colour as a property to an object. One dimension we call a 'line'. Two dimensions a 'plane', and three a 'space'. With time added, we call this a 'spacetime'. The problem with spacetime is that we are so used to thinking in three dimensions that we find it extremely hard to imagine an object in four dimensions. So what spacetime really is, is very difficult to imagine because our mind doesn't work that way! Try explaining to a line what a plane is. That is a step too far for a line. A line doesn't know about the existence of the 2nd dimension...

So spacetime is a mathematical model in which the 4 dimensions (length, width, height and time) can be described. This is necessary when we study the universe. Every object in space we actually see in 'history'. We see the sun now, but we don't see what it is like now. We see what it was 8 minutes ago, because light takes 8 minutes at 300,000 km/s to cover the distance sun - earth. So when you describe an object, you can give it an extra dimension: spacetime.

> According to Einstein, heavy objects can change the 'shape of space'. Instead of considering gravity as a result of mass attracting mass (Newton's law: mass 1 x mass 2 divided by their distance squared)), Albert Einstein calculates that space curves around objects of varying gravity. The greater the variation in gravity, the greater the curve. Light and time, which have no mass, will curve around the object and continue on its other side. A striking illustration of this is a bullet on a trampoline. The cannonball makes a pit in the surface of a trampoline, and if you put a golf ball next to it, it rolls towards the cannonball. So mass does not attract mass, according to this 'image', but objects just follow the curve of space. In a black hole, the curve is so strong that the golf ball 'falls' towards it.

This seems theoretical, but the theory of relativity also plays a role in everyday phenomena. Take GPS, for example, which allows you to determine your position on earth within a few metres. A GPS system receives information from satellites orbiting the earth in a fixed sphere. If you are standing somewhere on earth, your GPS searches for the position of the satellites at exactly that moment.

Two things are important here. First, satellites move faster compared to our resting state here on Earth (a larger orbit per 24 hours!). The satellite's time is therefore 7 microseconds per 24 hours slower than on Earth. But gravity also plays a role.

Satellites are located at a distance of 20,000 kilometres from Earth. There, gravity is four times less than on Earth's surface, which means time goes 45 microseconds faster. So correcting those two numbers, time on a satellite goes 38 microseconds faster.

That doesn't seem like much, but if you convert it into distance, 38 microseconds of time difference means an inaccuracy of almost 11 kilometres per day. Or, if we did not know the theory of relativity and could not correct the time differences, a GPS system would be useless!

The general theory of relativity is of enormous importance to our view of the world. For example, the Big Bang theory would never have come into existence without the theory of relativity. But especially for our own worldview, it is a shock! If my twin brother lived on another planet, with a different speed and gravity then he would only be 40 at the time of my 80th birthday, for example. Or... relativity has become the complete death knell for our western classical, static worldview.

And then, quantum mechanics was developing in Einstein's time...

Briefly summarised:

When we see objects around us, this seems to be a solid truth. Matter from that object does not just disappear suddenly. Yet Einstein showed that matter can be converted into energy and vice versa. Or you could say: matter is actually *compressed energy.*

Time also seems like such an established truth. Yet it has been shown that time does not pass the same everywhere in the universe. If you live on another planet (at twice the speed of Earth), you could celebrate your twin brother's 40th birthday on Earth on your 80th birthday....

And then space. The universe is huge. The end is where the furthest galaxies are. And then what is beyond that, if the universe were then some kind of giant sphere? We solve this by saying that space is 'infinite'. Infinite? Hello, try to imagine this...

Or... mass, time and space are 'illusions', attached to our earthly existence.

Chapter 5

The shocking of quantum mechanics.

Niels Bohr (founder of quantum mechanics): 'If quantum mechanics hasn't shaken you, you haven't understood it. '

Just as Einstein saw that our notion of the universe did not correspond to reality, Niels Bohr saw that certain phenomena within the atom also did not match our image of it at all...

Light is represented as a wave. A wave is a moving up and down movement of, for example, water (in the sea) , sound (sound wave), radio signals (radio wave)...etc. With this model, the progress of light can be explained perfectly. But light can also generate electricity, as in a solar panel. This is impossible to explain with the wave model. Einstein found the solution and showed that light also consists of energy packets or energy quanta (=quantity), we also call these light packets photons. So light is a stream of photons, comparable to a stream of marbles or particles. But... marbles don't wave! Or, those two models are incompatible. So it's like saying an object is coloured red, but also green at the same time! And that's not all. It was later shown that all basic particles within the atom sometimes behave as waves, sometimes as particles. Electrons are thus not at all like in our 'planetary' model described above (see chapter 3) with 'orbits', shells or energy levels. In the conditions of classical chemistry they behave like that. It's a 'model'. Perfect for use in classical chemistry.

As we saw in Chapter 3, electrons circle the nucleus in orbits or shells with different energy levels similar to the orbits of planets. Electrons can jump between those shells or orbits. Because each orbit has a different energy level, when they jump, a small amount of energy is released or absorbed according to the energy difference. Those energy packets are also called photons or quanta here. The movement (=mechanics) of those energy packets (=quanta) is described in a mathematical model. This set of equations was formulated by Max Planck and Niels Bohr and forms the theory of quantum mechanics. The outcome of these equations is bizarre. No one can *really imagine the* result...

Protagoras (485 - 421 BC): 'Every issue involves two lines of reasoning diametrically opposed to each other.'

Albert Einstein: 'There must be a deeper level of understanding that eludes our gaze...'

Until experiments proved that Einstein and most scientists of the time were wrong

Niels Bohr: 'Everything we call real is made of things that cannot be considered as real.'

Understanding the mathematical equations is not important to us. What does matter are the consequences of those equations recorded in experiments. The most important are the following:

1. Quantum entanglement

Particles (e.g. electrons, protons) that have been close to each other at a certain moment have an invisible bond: in the case of proven experiment, it is the spin. The spin is the magnetic direction of rotation of an electron. A spin is either up or down. It is a property, just like its mass, volume, charge... (that's all you need to know about it). If those two electrons are together (=paired), then each one has to have a different spin. Now that bond appears to persist even if the particles move away from each other. In principle, two particles on different sides of the universe would still 'know' of each other's existence. The moment someone then changes the spin of one particle, the other particle will immediately 'realise' this and adjust its state to that of the observed particle and show an opposite spin, when measured. Two 'paired' particles hundreds of kilometres apart remain connected and can transfer information to each other (**quantum teleportation**).

Quantum entanglement has long been controversial because the information exchange between particles is instantaneous, and therefore faster than light. This seemed physically impossible because the speed of light is the absolute maximum. Yet it has been demonstrated repeatedly over hundreds of kilometres in many experiments.

Albert Einstein: 'Ghosting at a distance is impossible!'

Quantum computers will become the next generation of computers if we can develop them further. They are based on this 'ghostly' principle.

2. Superposition

The particle has two states simultaneously (wave and particle) and 'chooses' only one state upon observation, when you measure it. The result also depends on the measurement. So an independent measurement of, say, an electron therefore does not exist. The particle keeps all possibilities open and only makes a choice when you measure it. And even then the result depends on how you do the measurement. The particle (or the wave) is also in many places at once, until you measure it....

3. Quantum tunnel effect

A particle is both particle and wave at the same time (wave-particle duality) and can thus break through energy barriers. For example: on the sun, two hydrogen nuclei collide. These nuclei are so small (see chapter 3) that they would hardly find each other. But the hydrogen atoms behave like waves and 'flow' over or through each other, as it were. The two nuclei fuse like particles into one particle of helium.

> Radio waves, sound waves... can pass through walls. We know that. But the bizarre thing is that particles you can represent in your imagination as marbles also pass through walls as waves. And they can then become marbles again afterwards....

In classical particle theory (solar system model), electrons move around. In reality, this is not so. A better representation of electrons is a diffuse, wave-like cloud of 'electronity' around a tiny nucleus: the 'probability cloud'. It is not surprising that they pass through barriers just like sound waves...

> **Louis de Broglie (nuclear physicist):** 'Everything has both wave and particle characteristics. '

The first and therefore most famous proof of quantum effects is A. Aspect's two-slit experiment: one electron 'flows' through two slits at the same time (bizarre, but wave effect!) and when you catch it on a screen you see one particle. When observed, it 'chooses' its nature, as it were. This choosing depends on measurement. When measured, the particle 'chooses' and this 'strange' property disappears. Electrons, but also protons, thus become 'real' only when we measure them. So, we know what happens, we can also calculate it, but we don't get it...

> **Werner Heisenberg (nuclear physicist):** 'What we observe is not nature itself, but nature exposed to our method of interrogation.'

Briefly summarised:
In classical chemistry, we represent the particles of an atom by little balls or marbles. Those 'marbles' have really bizarre properties that make the representation by a marble no longer sustainable. If we then try to represent the particles within the atom by a wave motion (such as a vibrating sound string, radio

wave or the wave motion of seawater), again, it does not correspond with all the experiments:
Electrons can

1. Be in two different places at the same time (quantum superposition).
2. Be wave and particle at the same time, and making a choice depends on your observation. (quantum superposition).
3. Pass through energy barriers (quantum tunnel effect).
4. Have 'Ghost-like relationships' persisting regardless of their distance (quantum entanglement).
5. In quantum entanglement, information can be transmitted 'instantly', even over long distances (quantum teleportation*).

Time magazine 14 July 2017:
Chinese scientists have successfully teleported an object from Earth into space, reports MIT (Massachusetts Institute of Technology).
Specifically, a photon particle was sent to a satellite orbiting the Earth at a distance of just under 500 kilometres. This 'sending' happened in... zero seconds! The breakthrough paves the way for more ambitious and futuristic projects. The technique the scientists used is called 'quantum entanglement': a 'strange phenomenon, which occurs when two quantum objects, such as photon particles, are created at the same time and place in space

and thus share the same existence', according to MIT magazine.

 A year ago, scientists managed to teleport an object outside a lab setting for the first time. 'In the past, experiments with teleportation were limited to distances of about 100 kilometres', say the MIT journal researchers.

Chapter 6

What are the consequences of relativity theory and quantum mechanics for classical science?

Classical science is based on two principles:

- Locality: if a particle or object is 'there', it cannot be anywhere else.

- Causal relationship: if you know all the parameters in a system, you can describe the consequences: cause and effect. The state of a system can only be changed by external causes. For example: a football is lying on the grass. It only can change its position by an external force, i.e. a kick. If you know the precise force (size, direction and point of contact on the ball) of your kick, you can calculate its trajectory and know where it will land.

In quantum mechanics, this is not so!

1. So is classical science wrong?

You cannot apply quantum phenomena to all particles. There must be a 'relationship' between those particles: they must be 'synchronised' (= tuned to each other: wave peaks and valleys must coincide, like in an MRI scanner; we call these two *'paired'* particles, e.g. electrons). We call this relationship, this connection, **coherence***. With decoherence the properties are lost. Maintaining this coherence is the difficulty in the tough development of a quantum computer.

Large objects (such as a football) consist of many billions of decoherent atoms. Therefore, quantum phenomena do not occur in large objects. The interplay of those billions and billions of particles is globally perceived as 'normal'. We observe averages of all the particles. But through more precise observation, we now know that the individual particles do not behave like this.

So you can certainly continue to correctly describe the movement of a football, a spaceship or the solar system with classical mechanical laws!

In chemistry, too, we describe millions and millions of particles at once. We can make wonderful use of their 'averages' in classical chemical laws.

We know that on Sunday evening, for the (mathematically) average Belgian from the coast heading inland, there will be a traffic jam on the motorway. We can describe the properties of that queue. For example, it has the same bottlenecks every week. (=classical mechanics) But this says nothing about my individual behaviour: I myself take the N 9 from Ostend to Bruges. My neighbour stayed at home. We are not in the traffic jam. Last week we took the highway, because we forgot it was Sunday evening, so we were stuck in traffic. Two other neighbours do take the motorway and find themselves in a traffic jam just before Bruges. Belgians seem to behave like 'average herd' (classical mechanics), but they don't. Everyone behaves differently (quantum mechanics!)

2. Is something alive a large object?

We have already seen in chapter 3 that just one gram of earthly matter shows more variation than all matter elsewhere in the universe known to us. And the most extraordinary thing of all is that life arose from it. Life is extraordinary…!

Blacky, my neighbour's cat walks by. He could smell me before he saw me. He also smells the flowers five metres away. He pricks up his ears: a frog is breathing among the reeds. Suddenly, he jumps forward to the edge of the pond and catches a fish. He runs away with it for miles. With the help of a cat friend, he can easily make creatures of the same species as himself, from the same materials that make up the stones around him. And our cat is just one of many living species capable of hundreds of these, and many other amazing feats. Some ants carry up to 30 times their own weight. The sidereal can generate a voltage of 600 volts. Birds travel from the north to the south of our globe as if it were nothing. Every green plant can build its plant body out of water (from the soil) and carbon dioxide (from the air) just like that (we call this photosynthesis).

And then... man! Man has one organ whose performance is second to none. Our brain far surpasses the capability of a computer. A computer does not yet come close to the fabulous ability of our brain on every level. That wonderful creativity has led to pyramids, highways, cars and the theory of relativity on our planet....

The whole wide variety of lifeforms on Earth is made up of the same atoms as the rocks around us or on Mars or the moon. How is it possible that, over time, something that can 'walk, jump, fly, sail, think, talk, desire...' was created from that matter on Earth? And not elsewhere (as far as we know)?

How is it possible? We ourselves have never made anything alive...

3. Let us take a closer and deeper look to the miracle of the living

Anthony Van Leeuwenhoek was a woolfabric trader. To check his fabrics for weaving quality, he used a magnifying glass. One day, to obtain stronger magnification, he had a revolutionary idea: he placed two lenses above each other (at a certain distance, to get the image sharp) and discovered that the total magnification of the lenses was not simply added, but multiplied! So two lenses of 5X magnification gave the object not 10X larger, but 25X. The first microscope was born. Out curiosity, Van Leeuwenhoek enlarged not only cloth but also all kinds of living material. It looked very different. Yet all that living was always divided into 'cubicles', just like the bricks in a wall, or the honeycomb of a bee. He concluded: all living things are made up of 'cubicles' or cells.

We now know that the basis of all life is the cell. Our body is composed of some 35 trillion of these cells. Each cell is extremely complicated. Hundreds of chemical reactions happen simultaneously. We can simulate almost all those reactions with complicated equipment in the lab, but each cell does everything at once, in just one millionth of a microlitre content. And it still has raw materials and energy left over to multiply. How is this possible?

Mortality is another mystery. All chemical reactions are reversible. In principle, also those of the cell. But no one has ever turned a dead cell into a living one. What is definitively lost when a cell, animal or plant... dies?

Nor can we make life. The only way is by injecting biochemicals into living cells, or by eating them to make part of our bodies. Why can't we do in the lab what the lowest viruses and bacteria do effortlessly in nature?

We still have a long way to go, but quantum mechanics can already give us a small hint. The quantum mechanics of life is in full research and will be revolutionised in the future. Some examples of already proven mechanisms:

The robin can detect weak Earth magnetism through quantum entanglement. One of the two entangled electrons on the outer eye membrane is slightly modified by the earth's magnetic field. The second paired electron inside the eye (retina) simultaneously receives that information and transmits it to the brain. Based on this, researchers were able to calculate that the 2 particles remain entangled for at least 100 microseconds. In a laboratory, they only managed to maintain the quantum state of electrons for 80 microseconds ...

All reactions in the cell are quantum-driven. Particles are everywhere at once, flowing like a wave through energy barriers (quantum tunnelling) and becoming 'particles' where they are needed in the reaction centre. We know this in classical chemistry as the action of an enzyme. They are needed in every vital activity. If we simulate those same reactions in the lab, we need much more energy because our reagents are not quantum-controlled, not coherent....

Cells are thus coherent in a way. This means that many (all?) parts are synchronised, or that information is present in all of them at the same time. The atoms or atomic parts of a cell do not fly around randomly, but have information from the rest. And they also behave accordingly. It is still a mystery how in living cells this coherence is sustained, because this is a condition for quantum control.

Photosynthesis is another proven example. It's an extremely complicated process by which a plant can make sugars and proteins from water and carbon dioxide to build its plant body. It is the reverse of burning (oxidation) by which we release energy. (see chapter 7.3) Again, quantum entanglement has been demonstrated here: particles flow as waves, are 'omnipresent' and react precisely and with the appropriate particle.

So one particle is everywhere at the same time, and thus somehow becomes 'aware' of the location of the other particle. Then it connects. We don't understand it, but the least you can say is that many chemical reactions in the cell are not blind coincidences, like the same reactions in our test tubes. (It is not a lottery with probability!) They are much more purposeful.

Briefly summarized:

The world around us behaves according to the laws of classical science but when we look deeper inside the atom, this is not so. Particles within the atom that are in tune with each other (we call this coherent) show bizarre properties. For example, maintaining 'ghostly relations' independent of their distance, or 'teleportation'.

If we greatly enlarge living matter, it always consists of 'cubicles, boxes' or cells (for example, as in a honeycomb). The cell, of course, is then again made up of atoms and is the basis of all life. Recent research shows that cells are coherent, so reactions in the cell are not fully explained by the 'blind chance' of classical science. Without superposition, teleportation and quantum entanglement, life is impossible. Particles 'know' something about each other, which means that everything in the cell runs much more efficiently than in our lab.

May I invite you, to focus on one object? Anything. Something you like. Or an object of use. For example, your ballpoint. Look how beautifully it is made . Many people have thought about it and made it according to the classical laws of matter. It takes iron, mined by someone, melted, forged. Plastic is a carbon compound. Petroleum was mined for it. All parts have been invented, improved many times and made. It is the fruit of the labour and thought of hundreds of people. All over the world. Feel gratitude that they have done that for you. See how it works, disassemble it. Focus on a small piece of that object. Focus on one point, one mm², no more. Close your eyes and go deeper into this small piece. Hold the image. Imagine the billions of atoms of this tiny piece of matter. And the little parts of those atoms: the protons, neutrons and electrons. They move like bees in a hive. Imagine their 5 ghostly quantum properties. Concentrate on them one by one. A wink, a smile at your mind... Their purposeful playfulness. Billions of particles play within you. That playfulness flows through you... You yourself are that play. Play, the nature of it all... Feel it inside you. In your throat, down to under your chest... Feel the energy of that play and remember now that that playful matter is actually 'solidified' energy and that time is a beautiful illusion.... We are energy and play on forever.

Chapter 7

How is it possible, that 'lifeless' matter ever produced 'life'?

1. The evolution of matter begins nearly 14 billion years ago with the big bang

We have looked into the structure of the matter in previous chapters. Let me recap: The universe is made up of three basic particles (protons, neutrons and electrons) that form the atoms. On Earth, 92 types of atoms exist in their natural state. But although atoms exist, you don't yet have matter. A 'mysterious independence' forms them and binds them together, as we discovered in quantum mechanics. Matter particles are temporary stacks of energy (see the section on relativity). Together, that matter forms a powerful system: our earth, planets, solar system and Milky Way. This is not an endless repetition, because each planet, moon or star is different. Yet each component within the system forms a total unit. Planets revolve around the sun at constant orbits according to Kepler's laws. The moon orbits the earth in 28 days, the sun orbits the centre of the Milky Way in 25 million years, comets form regular ellipses, and so on. Similarly within the atom. Each particle is different, but forms a total unit. So both the very small (atom) and the very large (universe) are woven as one, following the same method, but never repeating: in ever new creativity and playfulness. And... don't forget that this material system is actually only 4% of the universe we observe!

Not everything happens constantly and everywhere in that universe. Stars are the basic workplaces where the smallest atom of hydrogen is converted to a larger atom of helium (see Chapter 4). Later in that star's life, we then get conversions to carbon, oxygen or iron. The iron atom in your red blood cells, was made in such a star! The heavier atoms (with more protons than iron) were formed through nuclear reactions at the end of the life of a star, when he explodes (supernova). This 'stardust' formed our Earth, about 4.5 billion years ago, leaving us just under a hundred types of natural atoms on earth. But this is not all. Atoms also bond with each other: the molecules.

Molecules or atoms can form larger structures via geometric shapes, such as a pyramid, a cube.... We call this a crystal lattice. This means that the atoms then sit together in a fixed 'shape': pyramidal, cubic, hexagonal... Externally, we sometimes see this in a crystal. We all know its splendour. Here atoms sit together in a 'rigid' , fixed way in a geometric pattern.

But there is another way to form larger structures. A much more playful, creative possibility. We have some atoms with a 'half-filled' outer shell that can form long chains because they can 'bond with themselves' (see Chapter 3). Carbon is the most important one for us, but silicon (Si: the basic component of sand) is also one of these and is mainly used in electronics. We call such chains polymers*. The length and variety of those chains of equal carbon atoms is seemingly limitless.

So here we notice an evolution over time: atoms, molecules gradually get bigger, more complicated. First at the level of the atom: heavier atoms are more complicated than the light ones, such as hydrogen and helium. Then atoms form molecules. First simple ones like water, for example, but then bigger and bigger as time goes by. For classical science, all this is blind chance, a lottery. And so it seems 'on average', but we now know that quantum mechanisms come into play when 'separate' atoms meet.

So you can see from youthful earth that more complicated structures are formed as time goes by. Some are successful, some are not. Often a development with quick or 'immediate success' is a dead end. In the 'search' (the urge?) for larger structures, the creativity of the crystal is limited. But not the bonding of carbon molecules into polymers. There seems to be no limit on getting bigger and more creative with their long chains: There are more types of molecules with the atom carbon (studied in organic chemistry) than there are molecules with all the other atoms combined. Think of all living things, but also of all synthetics, plastics, etc.

The crystal structure is a beautiful experiment of nature. We can still see the rocks all around us. Most of the earth's crust consists of crystal structures. But the evolutionary process does not build on them. Through carbon molecules, however, evolution can take further steps.

Now let us reflect for a moment on that 'drive', that 'direction of evolution' that you notice from the beginning. Where does it come from? How can we explain it? Is it just a coincidence? We look back at recent scientific discoveries.
We thought mass and time were constant. But that is only seemingly so on Earth. We thought the location of continents on Earth did not change. But that is only seemingly so in the last few thousand years. We can now accurately measure the displacement year by year. Due to exceptions that we could not explain with the rules or laws in force at the time, we started to observe more closely. And now we know: every substance can basically give off radiant energy, every mass undergoes changes due to its speed, every particle has 'ghostly properties'... but on Earth the differences are often too small to see the truth. Or the number of particles is too large, so that we measure an average result. In this seemingly average stable world we have been brought up and reason and think. Our minds work that way too, and that's how classical science thinks about evolution.

Yet even Einstein never believed that all this could be created by blind chance. So how then?

In the last century, we have often found through 'strange' exceptions that the rules were completely different from what we originally thought. The situation here on earth turned out to be the exception to a much broader general law that sometimes looked completely different. Let's take a deeper look and for now, due to lack of evidence, follow our intuition. Particles (e.g. protons) can 'become aware of' (also changing) information from other particles. At least at that moment, therefore, they 'know' something that is vitally important for the functioning of a cell. This has been proven. If it did not have this information, the cell could not possibly work. We will constantly encounter this in further evolution. (The targeting of DNA mutations has also been proven, see later)

'Particles that know' is anthropomorphic, but how to find other words...?

> **Niels Bohr**, one of the two founders of quantum mechanics: 'We must agree that, when it comes to atoms, language can only be used as in poetry. '

We do not, of course, recognise consciousness in the 'knowing' of particles, atoms. We only clearly recognise consciousness in humans: human consciousness is a 'strange' exception for classical science.

Even in a human being, you can't measure consciousness, not even really define it properly, but of course you can clearly see its effects. It is perfectly observable, whatever definition you use. You can't ignore it.

But also in animals, you can't ignore this consciousness, this inside, can you? Anyone who studies behaviour of higher animal species like dogs or cats knows that there is a consciousness present. Is that awareness only reserved for mammals? Many people who keep parakeets are convinced that their pets have a personality of their own. Should we then include birds? Or do their common ancestors (the reptiles) also have consciousness? Does it stop there? You shouldn't tell this to aquarium enthusiasts. Those are convinced of the consciousness of fish or octopuses. Fish 'know' when their owner feeds them. Did consciousness then originate in the nervous system of their common ancestor, the jellyfish? And then in plants? Viruses? Bacteria? In a stone? Among atoms?

Through the 'exception' in humans, we have to face the fact that **everything** has an 'inside', a consciousness. Just as we observed in other phenomena. Only that inside, that consciousness, is not perceptible to us for the time being in, say, a stone. Relativity and quantum phenomena are also not observable in a football, yet they are present as we now know. The movement of continents is there all the time, although we couldn't observe it before.

There is another reason why it makes sense that everything has consciousness: the unity of the universe. The universe is built in the same way everywhere. A stunning unity. Man too is part of that unity. Man is not built different from the other parts of the universe. So why then would consciousness 'suddenly' appear in humans? Or in mammals? Or in fish? It is much more logical to assume that it is present everywhere, but not measurable in most places for the time being.

Already shortly after the Big Bang, 'below' that material layer, a layer of 'consciousness' must have been present. Outer and inner must match. The building materials of this nascent universe are virtually homogeneous at the origin. So is the consciousness that belongs to it. We can 'see' from the complexity of matter where consciousness is highest, greatest. It is like identical twins.

So if you accept this, you can simply see evolution as a rising, growing of consciousness.

Max Planck (nuclear physicist, the other founder of quantum mechanics: 'There is no matter as such. All matter arises from and exists only because of a force that makes the atomic particle vibrate and holds this 'little solar system' together. And behind the force that holds the vibrations of the atomic nuclei together, we must postulate the existence of a conscious and intelligent mind.

The things that organize the world are not pieces of matter, but essentially vibrations. These vibrations are not random, but coherent. (adapted)'

'I consider consciousness to be fundamental. We cannot ignore consciousness. I regard matter as a derivative of consciousness.'

David Bohm: The vibrations are informed. (they 'know' something)

25 February 2019, Varanasi, India

Suddenly, in the teeming crowd of people around me, a man lies unconscious. In fact, he almost gets trampled! I run towards him in a panic to straighten him out and keep the people away. But he is unconscious... A Hindu priest puts his hand on my arm:

- Let him. He has a drinking problem. He is sleeping off his fuddle.

- But you can't get alcohol here, can you?

- Not officially, no...! By the way, don't give anything to beggars either. They can usually work. It's not good for them to earn money like that. And for those who have nothing anyway: we give free rice breakfast every day, à volonté for anyone who wants it. May I invite you for breakfast tomorrow morning at the Vishnu temple?

From the next morning, I help in the Vishnu temple with the preparation and begging of the rice breakfast and often stay for a chat.

- Don't you see God in everything? The smallest mosquito, a person, a house, the asphalt you stand on... This demands respect!

I am deeply impressed. This Hindu priest knows that everything has an inside, a consciousness...

Consciousness, God, in that reasoning, is not something outside us. No, it's everywhere. Connected to the smallest atom to... man!

Guido Gezelle puts it this way (while admiring the movement on the water of a dragonfly) in 'Het Schrijverke' (The writer): In the poem the dragonfly answers the question 'what are you 'writing' on the surface of the water?':

'We write what us in early times

The Master-Creator told, coaching,

Just one lesson learning the primes;

We write, you can`t read, but we never knew

Why you couldn`t learn on the spot!

We write, we rewrite and we write anew

The Holy and Blessed Name of God!'

Now let us look further into the biological evolution of this consciousness.

We perceive that on our Earth, after about 3.5 billion years of growth, some molecules have become more complex. The most complicated are carbon compounds. Proteins, for example, contain thousands of atoms, starch too. DNA molecules even billions! They are the most complicated structure on our earth right now. So their awareness is also greatest if we accept this as two sides of the same coin. We face crossing a threshold...

2. 3.5 billion years ago: crossing the threshold of life.

In the morning my first job is making coffee. The growling kettle of water on the fire is a daily melody during the morning ritual . The fire adds a constant energy. This energy can be measured, but the water doesn't visibly change (if no gases such as oxygen are dissolved in it, because then you see little bubbles: the oxygen escapes because fewer gases can be dissolved in the water at higher temperatures). I only notice the effect of that added energy when I hang a thermometer in the kettle: 30°C, 40°C, 50°C, ... 90°C, ... 98°C, 99°C, 100°C. And I expect: 101°C, 102°C, ... But what happens: the temperature no longer rises, but the 'calm' water suddenly starts to swirl. Large bubbles escape, or of course you recognise this as 'boiling'.

So during the boiling process, you constantly add energy, but it is not visible in the water. Suddenly, at 100°C, it's noticeable (although you don't add more energy per time unit). This calm water suddenly has a visible explosion of power, crosses a threshold and takes on a totally different form: water vapour. The heat energy is the cause of this immense change. However, this energy was also almost completely present at 99°C, but it was not noticeable.

On Earth, carbon molecules are constantly becoming more complicated. They form long chains of thousands of atoms.

Their creativity is endless. External conditions (temperature change, UV radiation, volcanic activity, etc...) create a 'primordial soup' of very different carbon molecules. The internal energy of that primeval soup rises to a 'boiling point'. (Perhaps in several places at once, or as some claim via contamination from an impacting meteorite?) We 'see' this boiling point: life! We don't know when exactly and how such an organic molecule started 'living', but we see the effect. So it seems like a sudden transition, but it is not. We suddenly 'see' the effect.

> A pair of blackbirds has a nest in the hedge of our garden. From inside the house, we peer into the nest with binoculars. First, the female has laid blue-green eggs. After about two weeks, they hatched. Five beautiful blackbird chicks. But, after a few days, we see one of the chicks getting sick. We keep a close eye on it but do not intervene. Around noon, the little animal dies, much to our regret. We see it happen. Not five minutes later, the dead bird young is dumped. The mother immediately knows: this is no longer alive and no longer important. We too know what life is. We do not need complicated definitions, no measurements.

Life is a huge threshold, a new order. This is accompanied by a new level of consciousness. But the addition of internal energy remains the same: not a sudden thing, but a constant rise (like the heat energy at our cooking pot). We do not yet have measuring devices for this 'internal energy' although energy is usually measurable. Perhaps this is why energy is not a well-chosen term. That is why I will use 'inergy' from now on. (Compare: dark energy is also something so mysterious and unmeasurable, so is that energy? And from its elaboration in the universe, we also know it's surely there!)

August 16, 2006, Dassu - Gilgit, Pakistan
I turn 51 today and have slept badly. The atmosphere is below freezing. What are we actually doing here? I am annoyed with every pothole in the road. So this is constant. Our Belgian car is not made for this. It's crazy hot and I can't tolerate a Pakistani anymore. When you stop they come right out of the ground. It can't go on like this. Christine is much more resilient in such situations, but my rotten mood obviously works on her too. What do we do? Do we return? Do we go home? We have the choice. We oversee things. We have been travelling for 1.5 months now and have taken little rest. Heat, crowds, and all kinds of dangers weigh on you. We have never been away from home for so long. We long for our kids, family, friends...We knew it would be like this. We also travelled really 'basic'. If my mom could see where we all slept, I think she wouldn't sleep tonight. You have to be honest. A prison cell in Europe is cleaner and more comfortable.

Still, we decide to travel on and turn that page. I will no longer be annoyed by everything and everyone. Such an attitude must be dispelled! When will we be in Gilgit? Insjallah... But when we get there, we will call our children for my birthday and take a room to catch our breath for a few days.

We start again and take a hitchhiker with us. A very old Pakistani. A really sweet man. With gestures, he indicates the way to go. Yes, we know the road has been closed for 3 days due to landslides. A small path is free now. How can you get annoyed when you see the efforts the whole village is making in the blazing sun to keep the road open? (Or knowing how some Pakistanis sleep outside in our big European cities? Even our worst sleeping place was better than that in winter...).

Above our heads dangle boulders and rocks that could thunder down. At the next rain? Insjallah...
We slowly drive on. The man has a splitting headache. We share some food and drink. He chases children away. He has no sympathy for them. As a tourist, it is easy to give everyone something. Then you're off it, and your conscience is appeased. Financially it means nothing to you but you don't help them that way... What wisdom and gentleness comes from those sweet eyes... We get a warm handshake when he leaves us. His vulnerable gaze continues to travel with us. (see photo 3 on www.scienceandspirituality.be)
Yes, the inside exists... and is sometimes tangibly present.

3. 1.5 billion years ago: the revolution of the cell.

In the first billion years of life, we can unmistakably see the connection with non-living matter. Carbon compounds form primitive DNA molecules (in chapter 8, we take a closer look at what DNA exactly is) that can multiply along with some proteins: viruses. The earth is flooded with them. Later come the bacteria. They are a lot bigger and better organised. Species of both developments are still present on our earth. Think of the corona or flu virus, TB bacteria, yeast cells, yoghurt bacteria, etc. Bacteria still fulfil a hugely important role in nature or in our bodies. Without bacteria, the earth is not livable, even now.

> The first known life forms are fossilised microorganisms in hydrothermal sources, believed to have lived 4.28 billion years ago, not long after the formation of Earth: Precambrian stromatolites in the Siyeh Formation (Glacier National Park, Montana, Canada).

For a very long period, viruses and especially bacteria dominated the earth because the earth was unstable. There were also many times mass deaths due to catastrophes. One of them is well known: the oxygen crisis. Due to circumstances, for example mutations (see later), bacteria arose that could use carbon dioxide (CO_2) from the air (=photosynthesis) and thus oxygen (O_2) entered the atmosphere. Oxygen is a very dangerous reactive gas and therefore toxic to most bacteria at the time. They died en masse... And not only that. The increase in oxygen would eventually cause the complete ignition and destruction of the planet. A disaster!

For those who want to delve further into that chemical connection:

Carbon dioxide + water + solar energy→ carbon compound + oxygen released into the atmosphere

$$6CO_2 + 6H_2O \ (+ \ Solar \ energy) \rightarrow C_6H_{12}O_6 + 6 \ O_2$$
Carbon dioxide + water   carbon compound + oxygen

(=photosynthesis)

But still it did not work out that way. New types of bacteria arose that could use oxygen to make energy with carbon compounds: a kind of 'burning' (reaction with O_2) of carbon compounds ($C_6H_{12}O_6$): oxidation (like in a stove, to release energy). The reaction is: the carbon compound reacts with oxygen and becomes carbon dioxide and water.

Carbon compound + oxygen→ carbon dioxide + water + energy for cell operation

$$C_6H_{12}O_6 + \ 6O_2 \rightarrow 6CO_2 + 6H_2O \ (+ \ Energy)$$
Carbon compound. + oxygen   carbon dioxide + water
(=combustion or oxidation)

If you look closely at those two reaction equations, you will notice that the same atoms are passed over and over again on earth. We call this a cycle. But that also means that all parts of that cycle must remain in balance. Due to the development of industry, we burn a lot of fossil fuels (see second reaction equation). So more CO_2 is released into the air. This is not a toxic gas, but it does have the property of trapping solar heat like a blanket around the earth. This blanket is necessary because otherwise it might get -200°C at night. But it shouldn't be too much. In 1750, there was 0.0277% CO_2 in the air. In 2021, it will be 0.0440%. So we are making our blanket thicker! Consequence: the temperature rises...

So here, for the first time, we see a new evolutionary phenomenon: because of that mass death, bacteria that used oxidation came to full development and we see two types of bacteria emerging that complement each other perfectly: those who take carbon compounds from the environment for their energy and those who make with solar energy their own carbon compounds from the CO_2 in the air. The latter later become the green plants.

Over 99% of all organisms that have ever lived on earth have gone extinct. Over the course of our planet's history, new species have repeatedly occupied ever-changing biotopes, while older species slowly became extinct. But the rate of extinction of life on Earth has been far from constant. At least five times in the past half-billion years, 75 to 90 percent of all species on our planet disappeared from the earth surface in a geological instant during global disasters called mass extinctions.

Yet such a mass extinction is not a disaster for the evolution of the whole. Quite the contrary, in fact. Evolution just needed it. It makes space again for new, more creative species, accelerating evolution. Oxygen-producing species and oxygen-consuming species now form a perfect balance due to that catastrophe.

> Although mass extinctions were catastrophic events, they also created the ecological space for the emergence of new species. The mass extinction that has been studied most thoroughly, marking the boundary between the Cretaceous and Tertiary eras (the KT boundary, also known as the 'Cretaceous-Paleogene transition'), occurred around 66 million years ago and marked the end of all non-flying dinosaurs, creating room for the rapid evolution and diversification of mammals and birds.

That unstable period with emerging life lasts for millions of years. Nothing new seems to be happening, but the 'inergy' is rising constantly. Gradually, the atmosphere gets an oxygen quantity similar to now: because of the bacteria producing oxygen, the earth becomes more stable. In that searching mass of primitive life, all sorts of things are tried. Most attempts at further evolution are a dead end. But the 'inergy' is still rising... A wriggling mass of life, bacteria, viruses, mega-molecules... is at a turning point. And suddenly, 3.5 billion years ago, there it is: the cell.

> To develop a car, we used a pre-existing base: the steam engine (=bacteria). Steel and a horse-drawn carriage also existed. By combining the three, experiments were conducted to develop cars. The first cars were a curiosity and not at all reliable. Horses and carriages advanced faster! Most of the structures were failures, but gradually from those thousands and thousands of successful and failed structures, a stable, reliable car (the cell) emerged. All those stable cars have the same basic shape, yet the variety in functions, model, etc... is endless. From now on production is massive and easy.

Because the cell is so well built, it forms the basis of life. Its functioning is very complicated but phenomenal. Protein-based chemical reactions are controlled by quantum phenomena. The basic shape is the same for every cell, but the number of possible variations is endless. It forms the basis of all future life. Perhaps the transition to the cell occurred in many places at once but it happens only in one well-defined period. It is highly unlikely that the difficult and long transition from long carbon molecules to the cell as the basis for life took place multiple times. The entire primordial soup is not used, only a very small fraction of all possible molecules. There were countless more. All life uses the same type of protein, sugars and nucleic acids, (even the optical 'spin' is the same!) but most importantly the structure: all cells have the same parts, unity in diversity.

Meanwhile, many other primal forces are at work:

In 1915, Alfred Wegener noticed that if they moved, South America and Africa would fit together wonderfully. . It was also known from the study of living species on both continents that there must have been long-term contact between the continents in some way in the early history of mammals. Wegener went to investigate and also found that the rock layers in South America and Africa corresponded. He suggested that all the continents were once united into one big supercontinent and that the continents were still moving: continental drift. Unfortunately, he lacked a convincing explanation that prevented other geographers from taking him seriously. It would take until after his death for the mechanism of continental drift to become clear. Indeed, we can now accurately measure that America and Africa move away from each other by a few centimetres a year. And when two continents collide, mountain ranges are formed. The collision of the Indian subcontinent and Eurasia (India is even now shifting several centimetres a year!) causes the Himalayas to rise by a dozen millimetres a year. So Everest is getting higher to climb!

The eastern part of Africa is also currently tearing itself off from the rest of the African continent, forming a deep crack: the East African Rift Valley (from the Red Sea across Somalia to Mozambique) becomes 45 mm wider every year. This place seems to be a breeding ground for life and also the most likely place for the origin of man...

12 May 2007, Ethiopia-Kenya border region (see photo 4 and 5 on <u>www.scienceandspirituality.be</u>)

Around noon we arrive in Woito. We go to the local market. We move as inconspicuously as possible among the people and try to chat while buying something. Of course, as the only white people, you do stand out a lot, but after a bit of wondering, we are absorbed into the scene. Two tribes are present at the market: the Tsamai and the Buana, in their traditional clothing. Although there is often little real clothing here, apart from a beautifully decorated loincloth. Young men and women have beautifully adorned their slender black bodies. A feast for the eyes, and also very sexually charged. Yes, we are far away from all kinds of rules and regulations: sexuality, fertility, are so natural here. Part of everyday life, part of being human. People come to us and say hello very spontaneously, shake our hands. Some come to touch us. Especially the golden blonde hair on my arms intrigues them. I also feel their black arms. We sit down and taste the local sorghum drink. Now we are completely absorbed in that graceful mass... Christine has a way of taking pictures very discretely of this, for us, miraculous event. When we walk away in the evening, we are once again surrounded by children. What a life they have here compared to most European city children... Their eyes are two carbuncles of joie de vivre. We stroll further into the savannah and enjoy the sunset over this superb African landscape. Two boys are walking hand in hand with us while I look into their jet-black eyes. Their hand burns in my hand, I feel unified with the whole planet.

So many primal forces such as the earth's continental drift are still working continuously. But the parts of a cell now no longer build themselves directly from disorganised substances. **Pasteur** even showed that from a germ-free environment (without life), life can never arise...

> In the lab, we can simulate the situation of the young earth and also add the necessary atoms in this little lab-primordial soup. Organic carbon compounds are thus formed, but it remains lifeless matter. We cannot add the inside, the consciousness, the 'inergy'...? We have also discovered carbon compounds in the universe, but no life yet. It would be surprising if there is no life in this immense universe with billions of planets similar to our earth. But you can still argue that we may be alone in our solar system and that the rest of the universe is not bursting with life, let alone intelligent life.

The emergence of life is a unique, extraordinary event. There are not just cyclical events such as temperature rise and fall or mountain formation and then erosion back to plains. The earth is 'born', has a development and will also 'die'. During that development, certain influences are one-offs. Take the influence of the other planets in our solar system. We still know very little about their influence on Earth, but the latest discoveries suggest that their influence and location have been essential to Earth. (And who knows, even now, somehow, as is claimed in astrology) That situation lasts only for a certain period of time and does not recur: a 'one-time momentum' for the Earth. At that time, conditions were ideal, critical and unique. That transition was made only once. You can see this in the deep similarity of the cell structure of all living things. Life is a fundamental transition and is totally different from the substances of which it is built. It was born once and spreads like a lonely wave in the universe known to us so far.

Brian Cox (particle physicist and BBC programme maker) in 'The planets': 'Over the last decade, space missions have thought us a lot of new things. We used to think that our solar system was a standard system like thousands of others, but we have discovered that this is not the case at all. There are factors that have caused our solar system to develop in a unique way over the past 4.6 billion years. And we're only just beginning to really understand this. It turns out, for instance, that we are lucky the Earth exists (at all) anyway. The so-called 'Grand Tack Model' is a new theory that assumes that the great planet Jupiter spent millions of years destroying all space material around it as it moved more and more towards the sun. But fortunately, it was contained by Saturn's gravity before it could reach us. That there is life on Earth is also a matter of luck. Just ask Mercury, Venus and Mars. These at one point had the same chances as Earth to become habitable planets, but today Mercury is a scorched, arid planet, Venus a runaway greenhouse with a scorching atmosphere and Mars a frozen desert. '

And there is more. Cells do not live 'separately' but behave like a 'nebula', not separate 'lives' but a living membrane. All living things are interdependent: one makes oxygen, for example, the other carbon dioxide. They form an ecosystem and are connected into one big entirety: the biosphere.

So we notice that with each major period of development, a 'shell' or 'sphere' is built up. The Earth's surface mainly consists of simple atoms (oxygen, nitrogen...) They form the atmosphere and the hydrosphere (the totality of the water around the Earth: groundwater, rivers, glaciers, seas....). Rocks are a further evolution and form the lithosphere (only 80 km thick on average!) Those three spheres together form a stable whole for the biosphere: the entirety of all living organisms.

May I invite you to take earth in your hands. Feel and smell. Rub the earth between your hands. You don't see life, yet that tiny bit of earth contains billions of bacteria that ensure that the life we see can persist. Everything is connected. It's interesting to know that, but you also have to feel it. Close your eyes and focus on the feeling in your hands. Don't think anymore but feel the emotion, the gratitude. First in your head. Then let that feeling go down through your throat to your chest... Concentrate on that feeling. Breathe in and out. Your whole chest becomes flooded with that invisible wriggling mass... Immerse yourself fully in the pulsing of life...This life is also within you. You are it, yourself...

Chapter 8
The cell conquers the planet.

1.What is DNA and how does it work?

Although composed of stable atoms, life is physically unstable: without the constant addition of energy, living things instantly decompose into their composing molecules. But the cell has found a way from the very beginning to ensure the survival of 'the unstable', namely cell division: a cell can split perfectly into two 'younger copies', taking its entire hereditary material (DNA) with it into the offspring.

Anthony Van Leeuwenhoek already discovered that every cell has a 'dark spot': the cell nucleus. With better microscopes, a kind of 'coloured threads' or chromosomes (chromos = colour) were later discovered in that nucleus. They lie in pairs. The number of threads is characteristic of each living species. A fly has 12 (i.e. 6 pairs), an onion 16, a frog 26, a rabbit 44, a human 46... chromosomes. Later research under the electron microscope shows that each separate thread is actually a tightly coiled spiral. (double helix). Such a coiled spiral is in fact one large molecule: a DNA molecule. One DNA molecule, then, is made up of thousands of smaller sub-molecules: the nucleotides. There are only four different nucleotides and we now know that the order of those nucleotides is unique in every living creature. So the sequence of those nucleotides is a 'code' that represents hereditary characteristics. This is the construction of our own body with also some characteristics of parents, grandparents...

Several hundred nucleotides are needed per body characteristic (eye colour, hair colour, blood type...). Such a group is called a gene. Each human cell contains about 20,000 genes in its nucleus, because every single cell of our billions of cells contains the complete genetic code. A skin cell also has in its nucleus the building plan of your lungs, your nose, your heart... A small piece of hair or some saliva or a fingerprint leaves a few cells and is enough to find out your unique code in a genetic test. A super ingenious system! Different for every living being. But the same system for all life: again, that unity in diversity.

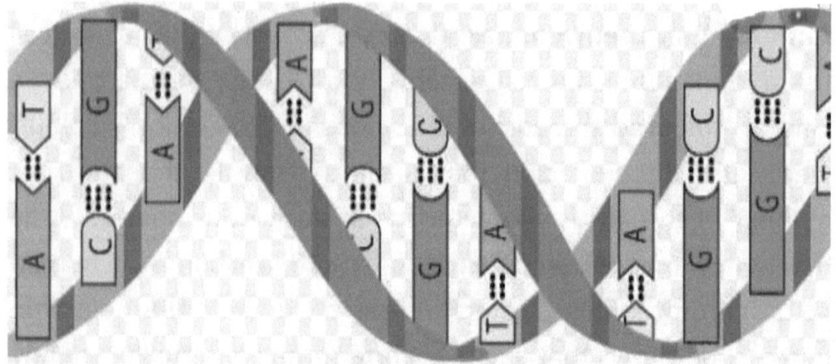

The DNA in the nucleus is a double helix. A, G, T, and C represent the 4 types of nucleotides. The dots represent the bonds between the two strands. When the bonds of the helix come loose, an exact copy is made in an instant on the two separate strands, so that each daughter cell carries a complete DNA with it in the cell nucleus.

Such a cell division is exponential: after ten cell divisions already more than one million cells, after twenty cell divisions in a favourable environment, the single cell can cover the entire earth! We now know this from the lightning-fast spread of the coronavirus.

> A Chinese legend clarifies what exponential growth means. The emperor of China was so delighted with the game of chess that he offered the inventor a reward. The inventor was allowed to choose whatever he wanted, except of course, the empire. The shrewd inventor asked for one grain of rice on the first square of the chessboard, and two on the second, four on the third, and so on, until the 64-squareboard was full. 'What a modest man!' thought the emperor at first, and ordered some rice to be put on the board. But the inventor outsmarted the emperor. Continuing the exponential trend - such as one grain on the first square, two on the second, four on the third, and so on - the last square of the chessboard requires the gigantic area of twice the Earth.

This is amazing but what is most surprising: the offspring are also completely renewed, they are younger!

> **Pierre Teilhard de Chardin:** 'Once the game of division of the nucleus is set in motion, nothing can stop this devouring fire of 'building activity from within'.'

2. What are mutations?

The coldest place on Earth is not one of the poles, but a place 1,300 km northeast of the South Pole in Antarctica. The lowest temperature ever recorded on Earth has been measured there: -89.2° C! You would think that no life is found there, but that is not the case. Beneath the 3.6 km-thick ice shelf is a freshwater lake, 250 km long. Completely cut off from the rest of the earth, a sealed microcosm for millions of years. Antarctica was once a much warmer place, bursting with life. So it was super interesting to investigate what happened to that life, when environmental conditions changed. Had all life been destroyed? Or was it possible that creatures had adapted to the extreme conditions: 300 X normal pressure, very low temperature, volcanic activity and complete darkness. The discovery of the lake became even more significant because the space probe Voyager 2 discovered a liquid ocean under the ice of one of Jupiter's moons (namely Europa) in 1980. Similar circumstances, in other words. The first careful drilling was carried out in 2012. The result was astonishing:

'We found no big surprises, most organisms normally live in freshwater in other places. In addition, the majority are species found in sediments of lakes or oceans'.

All DNA was almost identical to the DNA found in the rest of the world. Or: the DNA was copied and passed on flawlessly for millions of years, even in those extreme conditions!

All cells of higher animal species, plants... continuously use the system of cell division to renew their bodies, to grow... Those cells are an identical copy. In the system of sexual reproduction in higher species, you get different offspring but that's because the offspring gets half the DNA from each parent, and puts together a 'new combination' from that. The DNA itself remains unchanged.

It is therefore very exceptional that mistakes are made when passing on DNA to the offspring. When this happens, we call it a mutation.
Mutations are also necessary because otherwise you cannot have evolution, you would stay with the same species over and over again! If those changes provide new characteristics and an advantage for survival, then those cells have more offspring. They soon dominate the old species. (Think of the different corona variants: the most infectious one soon prevails) This mechanism was discovered by Darwin: natural selection.

3. Are mutations accidental or are they at least partially steered?

The big question now is: are these very exceptional changes in DNA a blind coincidence, or are they controlled? At least we humans can direct and change DNA.

> Genetic engineering or modification means that humans themselves change DNA in plants, animals or...humans. Through CRISPR/cas9 technology, this has become reliable and easy. This could be a boon for humanity. What about potatoes that are resistant to potato blight, or cereals that make their own soil nitrogen, like beans and peas do in nature? (This would make artificial fertilisers unnecessary) But a great danger also lurks around the corner: in 2018, the first two genetically engineered children were born with CRISPR/cas9. This led to global unrest and protests among biotechnologists and politicians. The Chinese responsible scientist ended up in jail.

So we humans can do it, but are DNA changes or mutations also controlled in nature?

The chance that by blind chance nature can create a simple molecule that can copy itself (this is nowhere near DNA!)

without guidance is one in 10.....(with 109 zeros). So in your primordial soup, you should have at least this number of molecules. But... this is a much larger number than even the number of elementary particles in the universe, and of course much larger than that of Earth! Earth did not have enough material or time to form such molecules by chance....

4. That steering occurs with mutations is so logical, but can we actually prove that steering?

In 1988, geneticist **John Cairns** did a curious experiment: millions of cells of an intestinal bacterium were inserted into a petri dish that contained only milk sugar (lactose) as a nutrient. An error had been introduced into one of the genes of those bacteria, which made it impossible for them to eat milk sugar. So they starved to death. Great was Cairns' surprise when new colonies appeared after a few days. Each colony consisted of offspring of bacteria that had managed to change their DNA code to eat lactose.

John Cairns showed that mutations in his cultured bacteria were partly caused by difficult environmental conditions and not by chance alone. It caused much disbelief in. However, the experiments were repeated and confirmed many times by others. A number of mechanisms have also been discovered, but certainly not everything has been fully explained yet (In technology, this knowledge has already been applied by developing bacteria that can digest leaked petroleum).

For us, it is important to keep in mind: evolution is not a sequence of 'coincidences', but a 'coordinated dance' between an organism and its environment. A 'dynamic' quantum mechanical process through which organisms continuously adapt to circumstances. This process is accidental and purposeful at the same time. Or... two opposites are operating simultaneously! We already know that this is not strange in quantum mechanics...

You can compare it to brainstorming when solving a problem. Ten, twenty, a hundred ideas randomly appear on the table before the right 'eureka idea' pops up. Another group will have completely different 'haphazard' ideas to arrive at that same (or a different?) best possible solution. After the solution, the brainstorming stops.

So yes, evolution is a haphazard process, but that randomness has a purpose. We know this because the process stops abruptly once the appropriate mutation is found in Cairns' bacteria.

Why is it that when you look for something, it's always in the last place you look (because then you stop looking!)?

Imagine a station hall at rush hour. Everyone seems to be scrambling disorderly. Mathematically averaged this is correct. But if you look at the individual travellers, everyone has a specific destination, a purpose. If there is a sudden fire alarm, this 'disorderly scrambling' totally changes, to another 'scrambling' that is also purposeful: getting away!

Another example to illustrate the interplay between chance and purpose:

You just happened to meet the woman of your life on the train. What a stroke of luck! Pure coincidence. You had been travelling by train every day for years. You sat in front of a woman reading a book hundreds, thousands of times. But the title of this particular book triggered something in you. You spoke to her and one thing led to another...

Is this really such a coincidence? Subconsciously, you prefer to sit with a beautiful woman not older than you. A woman alone, not a chattering travelling companion, also able to read a book quietly. And you were always interested in what the traveller in front of you was reading, whether it was your interest too.... Or: This encounter is not that coincidental! Coincidence and direction play together here!

So now you can see the earth like this: an immense primordial soup of virus-like organisms, bacteria and unicellular organisms. The unicellular organisms have the upper hand because they are better organised. So they have a better chance to survive. After the difficult start of life, this is a mega-success. The earth is 'overcrowded' with single-celled organisms. Even today, many representatives of this stage are still alive: single-celled seaweed, slipper animalcule or paramecia (no doubt viewed through the microscope in biology class), malaria... etc.

Chapter 9

The rebellious expansion of the biosphere

1. Simple but ground breaking : 600,000 years ago, multicellularity emerged

There is now single-celled life everywhere, billions and billions of living organisms crowding each other in the struggle for existence, natural selection. Looking only at the individual, this is the full explanation.
By multiplying so strongly and through mutations combined with natural selection, life protects itself. Trying everything to find everything...

But, we already know that there is more. Mutations are not blind chance. They are quantum-driven. The wriggling scanning of those expansion possibilities is not a blind coincidence, but targeted, because the inner inergy is constantly increasing via constant addition over time! The living single-celled mass comes to a boiling point again: consciousness and outer form must follow: 2.1 billion years ago, cells began to cooperate and form multicellular organisms.

That transition to multicellular organism can still be made in the lab even now, so it is not as exceptional as the transition to life. The 'drive' towards multicellularity is still present in a lot of unicellular organisms today.

> **Matt Herron** exposed algae to paramecia (slipper animalcules). Paramecia are single-celled creatures that eat single-celled algae, but not multicellular organisms. Herron says two out of five experiments this way produced multicellularity within half a year (600 generations). Other types of experiments also made the transition.

In the beginning the clusters of cells all the same, or at least roughly so, like a bunch of tightly packed grapes. You can still see this in the group (phyla) of sponges, animals still existing at this stage of development. There is still little cooperation between the cells, but the better protection from the environment is an advantage, and because of this advantage over the single-celled organisms, this 'sponge stage' is now the dominant species on the planet.

That doesn't take long. The 'inergy' rises further... The mass of sponges that fully populate the earth are searching, feeling, trying, exploring... and there's the next step.

2. Two layers of cells cluster around a cavity. The first laws of evolution reveal themselves to us

The outer layer of that cell cavity provides protection. The inner layer digests the food. A revolution, because now food particles larger than one cell can be taken up. Corals, jellyfish and sea anemones are the now living representatives of the phylum of the cavity animals.

To schematise the development of cave animals, the development of a human embryo can be viewed:

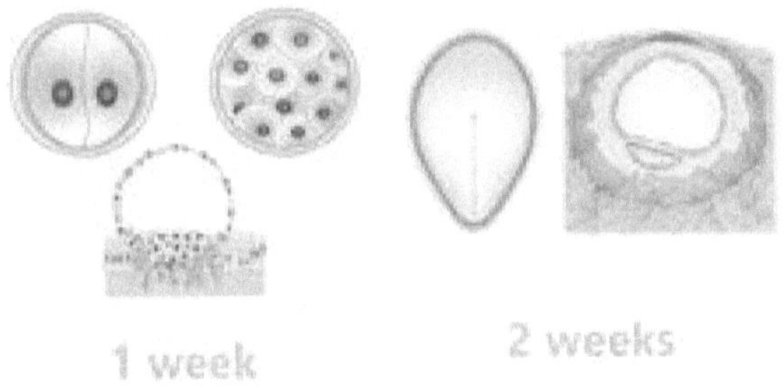

Schematically, this is the same. After one week, one cell has implanted itself. Above, you can see two cells after a first cell division. Next to it, a cluster of similar cells: the sponge stage. After two weeks, we get two cell layers around a cavity. We ourselves also experience this evolution at an accelerated rate : again, that enormous unity of everything (and the most beautiful evidence for evolution). The engine of evolution is now in full swing. It took us a good two billion years to get to this stage. We still have 600 million years to go until today...

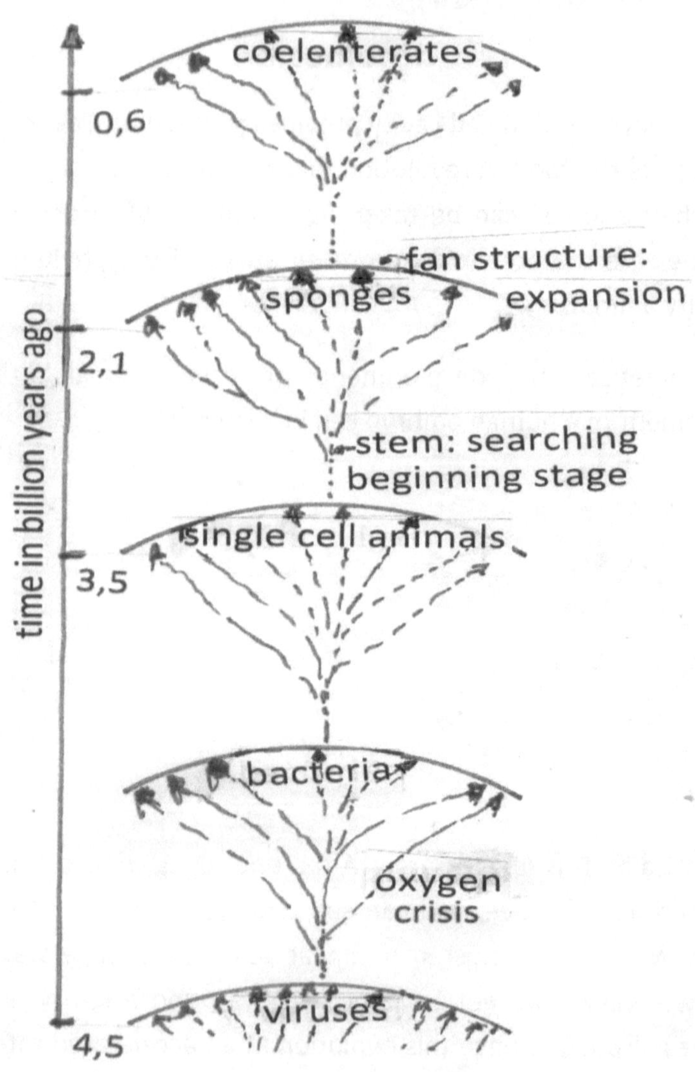

The emergence of life is laborious. In the beginning, it is searching, trying (first cars): the stem of the fan structure in the picture above. But all that searching eventually yields results: a successful form emerges. Single-celled organisms conquer the earth: a range of species in immeasurable numbers (the modern car): the fan structure: expansion. Yet the search does not stop because the 'inergy' continues to rise: cells begin to cooperate. Again hesitantly at first (the stem), then successfully: a second range displaces the first (fan). As the 'inergy' constantly rises further, the feverish search in that group continues: The cooperation of cells increases by dividing tasks. They group around a cavity.

The success of the new shape displaces the previous one (a new and better type of engine displaces the previous one in our car). Sometimes a 'disaster' helps get something better. Help! Toxic oxygen is created and almost all species disappear. There is room for the next thing.

This is only what we see outwardly. The real change happens inside: increase in 'inergy'. The external is a consequence. Again, we see the beautiful unity here: all living beings use the same DNA. Only 4 'puzzle pieces' are needed to pass on all the information. Those puzzle pieces, in turn, are composed of the same atoms as the universe. Only three particles make up everything: protons, neutrons and electrons. Yet unlimited creativity and diversity is possible: from rabbit to oak tree to human to octopus... Amazing...! Evolution happens all over the planet and forms the biosphere (global).

We can now easily derive the first four laws of evolution:

Law 1: Organisms become more complex over time.

Law 2: They form a unity in diversity.

Law 3: Development is global. A 'sphere' is developing.

Law 4: A crisis gives new opportunities.

> Even in a catastrophic mass extinction, life is not lost. Very much the opposite: evolution emerges stronger from the crisis. Just like it was necessary.

It is inevitable that the 'inside' has the same characteristics and corresponds to those of the outside.. We see an *ascent of consciousness*. In something living, this consciousness is perceptible to us. A jellyfish has a higher consciousness than a virus or a slipper animalcule.

Because most of the species have disappeared, it seems that there is no longer any connection between the separate species. Moreover, the numbers in the initial phase of a species (the stems of the fan structure in the drawing above) are very small. Only some of the broad end stages of the species can sometimes stretch their existence to now. We are not even aware of most of these species because no fossils have survived. Very small organisms almost never give a serious imprint in a rock or have no hard skeletal parts that can remain. So it is very difficult to find fossils. We know less than one millionth of the species that once lived...

If we were to dig up fossil cars within a billion years, the chances are almost non-existent that you would find something from the developing early stages of the automobile. At the time of their development, the number was very small compared to mass production today. So with a bit of luck, we would dig up cars from the current generation, but it is much more likely that everything has rusted up in the soil and we won't find anything at all!

3. The cool evolution from the jellyfish stage (cavity animals or coelenterates)

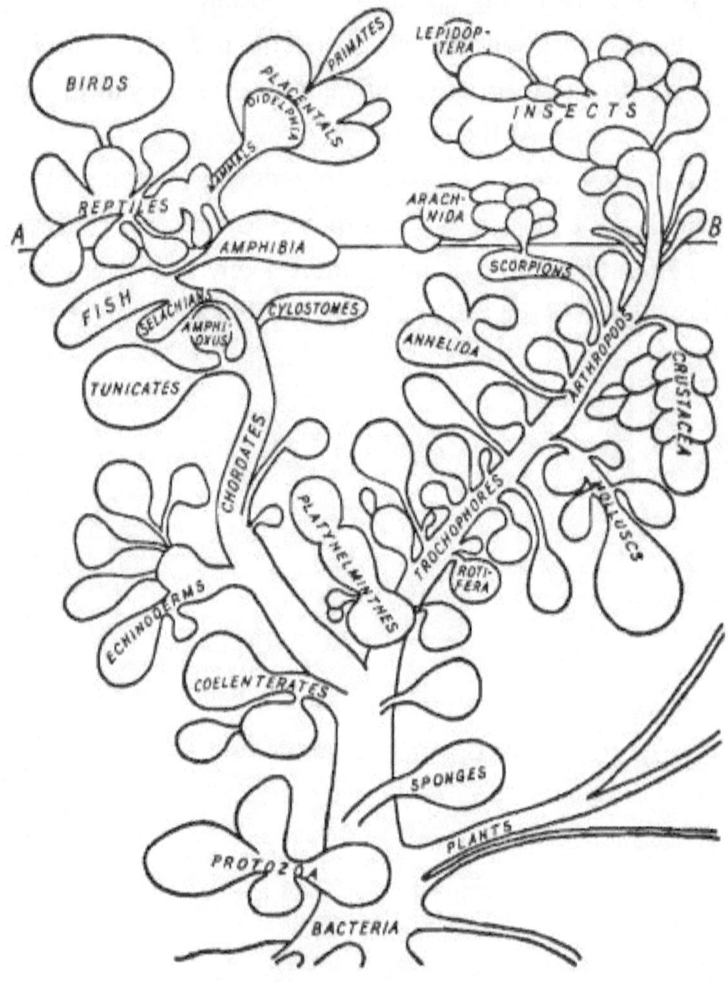

Take a good look at all the 'branches' on the family tree of life. We notice that animals and plants develop differently from bacteria onwards. But in unity: here, too, the cell is the basis. In green plants photosynthesis takes place in the cells. This is necessary to keep the biosphere in balance: carbon dioxide from animal life is converted back into oxygen and water, and (with their bodies), plants form new carbon compounds as food for animals (see above). Plant cells are sturdy because they have a thick cell wall. They don't need a skeleton like animals do. The evolution of plants is super fascinating, but we do not study this further. You notice the separate branch in the 'tree of life' of Cuénot (extract from 'The phenomenon of man', Pierre Teilhard de Chardin).

From 'the cavity animal' stage onwards, animal development splits into two major directions: those who 'choose' an external skeleton (the invertebrates) and those who 'choose' an internal one: the vertebrates. Notice also the AB line: this is the transition to land life. Life on land is more difficult. Temperature fluctuations are much greater, but dehydration in particular is the big challenge. Life already has to be well organised to 'take the water in and between the cells' onto land. Did you know that we also consist of almost 70% water?

May I invite you to choose a tree. Maybe one that is special to you. Or maybe not. Maybe just because you find it beautiful. Or because you notice that this little tree is struggling to survive in the forest among the many other large trees. Or because you had a sudden good idea in its surroundings. Perhaps a hunch that showed a new trend in your life afterwards... Look at its reaching branches. Its palms to the sky, fingers open, to the cosmos. Feel with your hands at the trunk. Feel every healed wound, every unevenness. Growing pains in his life. Feel the connection to the earth. Become part of it. Embrace that trunk and feel...Think of our long evolutionary history together. But then above all, let the wind in your face carry all thoughts. Feel your breath in your chest. Out and in, against the tree. Out and in...You become one...The branches take everything in your chest to the cosmos, the roots to mother earth.....

4. The rebellious ingenuity of the invertebrates

We only look at the representatives that remain today. (Over 99% of everything that was once alive is extinct!) In flatworms or platyhelminthes (e.g. a tapeworm), all cells are still close to the external surface. Cells can still breathe, digest, etc...autonomously here.

Cells of round worms need much more cooperation, but the segmented worms or annelids (for example: an earthworm) are a milestone! They are organised into parts or segments. (The rings on the earthworm you see). The cells digest nutrients together in a central digestive system and already have a transport system with a kind of 'blood' and 'hearts' to bring those digested substances but also oxygen to each cell. They have muscles to propel themselves along with tiny spines that lock into the soil as they move.

Those little spines develop further into legs (more efficient!) in the multipedes or polychaetes (example: a centipede). Those legs are not always useful. In crustaceans (crab, lobster, shrimp...) 2 X 5 remain. The rest develop into antennae, feelers, etc. Spiders and scorpions are even better organised: 2 X 4 legs. Meanwhile, the external skeleton ensures that the animals do not dry out and so the transition to land could also be made.

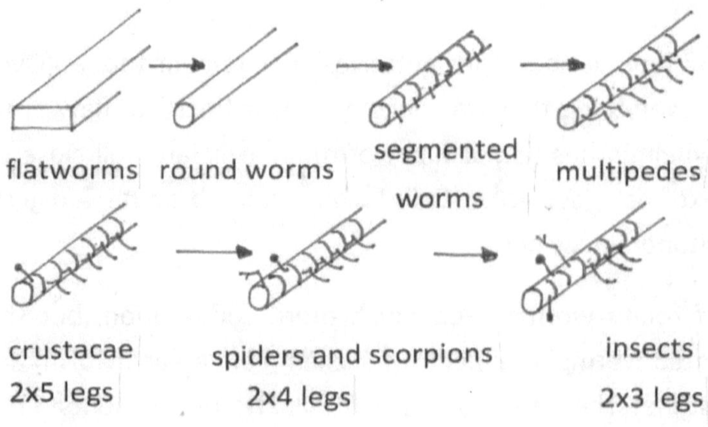

Insects are the final stage among invertebrates: 2 X 3 legs. The creativity of insects is grandiose: butterflies, ants, mosquitoes, flies, bees... The evolution in invertebrates is again super interesting, but in itself a biology curriculum for one year in secondary school education...

It is not difficult to see that the 4 laws of evolution that we already formulated in chapter 9.2 can be followed well throughout that development. But there's more. In the case of insects, there is not only better cooperation between the cells, but the animals themselves also work together! (This is certainly seen in vertebrates) A revolution: specialisation and cooperation increase the chance of survival. This can go very far, such as in bees or ants.

A colony of honey bees works so well together that they can almost be considered a single organism. This is bizarre: a colony can consist of a queen, up to 60,000 worker bees and about 1,000 drones or males. When a bee colony gets too big, the queen flies away from the hive. In this case, about 60% of the colony will fly with her to establish a new colony somewhere else. Meanwhile, the bees left behind give royal jelly to only one of the fertilized eggs so that this egg develops into a new queen. Each individual bee has a task that contributes to the well-being of the whole colony. A bee colony has one queen: she lays as many as 200,000 eggs per season. To do this, the queen receives sufficient energy and protein thanks to her diet of royal jelly. This is a glandular product of adult worker bees. Worker bees are also produced from the fertilised eggs. These eggs, unlike the queen, are fed on honey and pollen. Worker bees do all the work, but do not lay eggs. Larvae are completely dependent on the constant care of adult bees. A worker bee has a lifespan of 35 to 40 days in the warm season. Of these, she does about 20 days indoor service (cleaning, feeding, heating, ventilating) and 20 days outdoor tasks (tracking and collecting). Male bees or drones develop from unfertilised eggs. A drone mates with the queen. This happens during the nuptial flight.

We can formulate a new law here: the further the development, the more social animals become. Something essential in nature.

Law 5: The more advanced the development the more socialisation.

Chapter 10

Vertebrates keep all options open and therefore become a mega success

1. Fish (pisces) show all that is already present in aptitude for the entire group of the vertebrates

3 December 2006, Ko Lipe, southern Thailand
I have seen hundreds of films about the marine life in this area, but cannot believe it is so beautiful! It moves to the depths of your soul. I think of my two grandfathers who spent their lives at sea. They never saw this. A feeling of gratitude wells up in me from that encounter with the profound beauty of our planet... It is the same with Christine. We stand stunned, swimming from one coral reef to another. Sea apples with moving spines and fluorescent eyes, swaying sea anemones living in symbiosis with white-orange striped fish, grey fish with purple fluorescent tails, cup sponge, blackball sponge. Lemon yellow and intense

blue-striped fish, bottom crawlers with their camouflage colour... And all this in a peace and harmony that you can probably only find underwater. As a biology teacher, slides or film can't ever convey so much beauty to your pupils....

In evolution, fish are the first group of vertebrates. If we follow the fish in depth on the tree of life to see where they came from, there is a huge gap to the coelenterates (see Cuénot's figure above). This is because before the fish, a skeleton is missing. Skeletal parts already form exceptional fossils and without it it's nearly impossible. No representatives of those transitions have survived either. We know of only one small creature that has a bit a sort of spine: the lancelet.

Lancelets are transparent fish-like creatures up to 5 cm long. Fish-like, because strictly speaking, they do not belong to fish or even vertebrates. This is because they have no protective spine around their dorsal nerve, a typical feature of vertebrates. They are also called headless due to the fact that they have no clearly defined head. Limbs are also missing. They live in the sandy bottoms of shallow seas, their heads always protruding above the sand to filter plankton from the water.

But despite the lack of fossils or representatives, we can reconstruct evolution through the development of the embryo of other vertebrates. Each individual goes through the evolution of its species during its development. So through embryonic study, we do have a clear view of that evolution.

On the great 'fan structure' of cavity animals, evolutionary branches develop: disorderly, wild evolutionary twigs. Trying, trying… Until finding an 'impetuous fermentation' from which only one 'branch' develops further in a few million years. This becomes the stem of the fish's new fan structure .

One of those try-outs that did not develop further but of which we still have some representatives left are the echinoderms (e.g. the starfish). They are feverishly trying out a 'water vascular system'. This system creates water pressure in the many little feet at the underside of a starfish and is thus the oldest hydraulic system! You can compare it to the grab arm of a crane, but in a crane, the hydraulic system works with oil.

350 million years ago, the water was packed with invertebrates and fish (they predominated).

The 'inergy' is rising. The first insects are already on land. There is room and much more oxygen in the atmosphere (as much as 30 X more than is dissolved in water!) to make energy from food. Organisms are constantly becoming more complicated. The outwardly more complicated form is what we see, but we already know that greater consciousness corresponds to this.

Fish try out all kinds of things. Looking at today's fish, we find that some are able to survive the dehydration of the pool by taking in air in their digestive system to absorb oxygen. But the most successful attempt to take in oxygen is found among mudfish. They use their swim bladder (regulates the mass density of a fish, allowing it to float in the water) to take in oxygen from the air. This allows a mudfish to move to another pool by land. That swim bladder then also grows into a veritable lung in amphibians. (e.g. a frog).

On the mighty fan structure of the fish, many, many 'branches' again grow. Disorderly and wild. Some successful, others not. The water vascular system of the starfish is not kept in the further evolution. In fact, something better has been found in another evolutionary branch: 4 limbs with 5 thin protrusions: fingers and toes. This scheme appears to be the very best from the many trials. That branch continues to grow to the stem of the next fan structure.

The scheme that first emerges among amphibians is so phenomenally good, leaving so many possibilities for creativity, that it is retained in all later vertebrates. Also in humans (see comparative figure p.139).

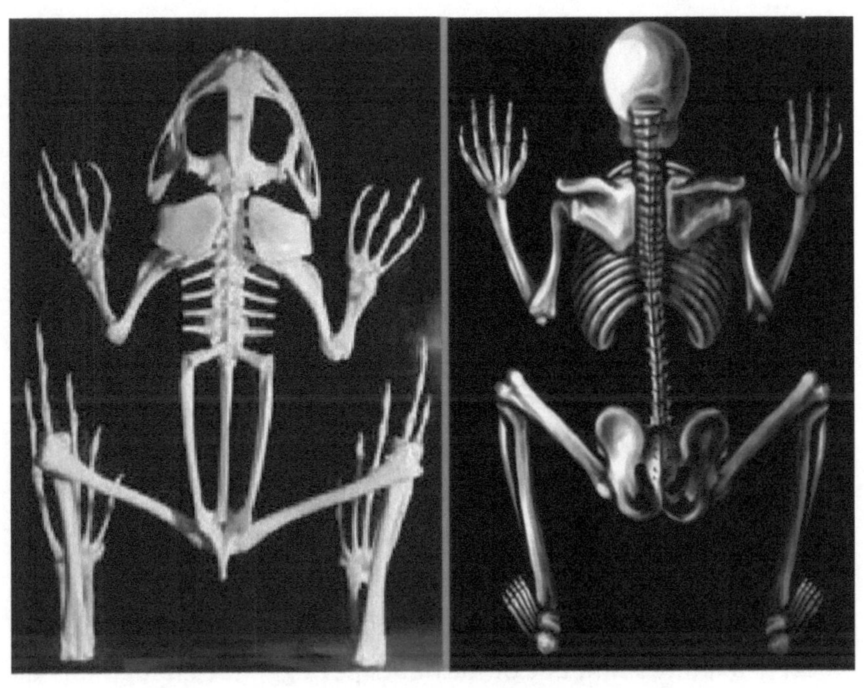

Comparison of limbs in frog (1) and human (2)

2. Amphibians hesitate to come on the land

The 'inergy' pushes and pushes... trying and trying. New forms emerge and then disappear again... Some fish are already half land-based. Other species are already partially adapted to land life. But the internal pushes the external forward. If not immediately, then step by step. An amphibian's eggs are laid in water. They would dry out on land. A lot of eggs are also laid because most sperm and eggs are lost through external fertilisation: frogspawn. Such a large quantity of eggs can only carry a limited amount of nutrients per egg, not enough for full development into amphibians.

What happens next? Every frog goes through the evolution of its species like any other living thing, but when the development of the embryo reaches the 'fish stage', the nutrients are used up. He is born as a fish (tadpole)! We call this a larval stage, and are amazed that this little fish is something totally different from its parents! In the larval stage, the little fish can take in food and fulfil the final step itself: becoming an amphibian.
So the larval stage is a system that circumvents the shortcomings of the reproduction system at that moment in order to be able to take the next evolutionary step! Due to the 'urge' on the inside, the next evolutionary step is taken, but the

body cannot yet follow. We see very clearly here that the inside comes first, and it gives impulse to the outside.

Amphibians are not yet true land animals. They remain bound to the aquatic environment through their reproduction. But also through their skin. A frog's lungs (developed from the swim bladder of a fish) are not sufficient for all the oxygen intake. A frog breathes mainly through its moist skin. That skin must be kept moist through regular contact with water. A frog is thus bound to the water's edge.

Amphibians have not just broken the prison of water, but are 'trying' to break free from it completely. We notice this especially in the many salamander species. Let's take a closer look at reproduction in the fire salamander:

> The mating season of fire salamanders falls between March and October with a clear peak in July and August. Mating occurs on land. Unlike in water salamanders, no eggs are laid but the fire salamander keeps the fertilised eggs in its fallopian tube (oviduct) to protect them. That is also where the eggs hatch. Complete larvae are thus given birth, which are already 2.5 to 3 cm in size at birth.

The Amazon frog looks for another solution:

> In the Amazon, it rains every day now. A little rainwater remains where the leaf is attached to the stem of the bromelia (the leaf axil). When an Amazonian frog female comes and wants to lay eggs, the male leads her to such a

'leaf axillary pool' . If she approves the puddle, she lays her eggs, one to six of them, and he fertilises them. After that, the father takes care of the rest. He guards the eggs and when they have hatched after two weeks, he takes the young tadpoles one by one on his back to a new leaf-oak pool. The tadpoles each get their own puddle as they would otherwise eat each other. The puddles do not dry out before the tadpole has legs. They must also contain enough food: leaf litter, algae and small insect larvae. They grow up there and after three months they turn into little frogs that leave the leaf axils.

We notice in those two examples that the further search for 'better' in reproduction, moves in two possible directions. The first solution is to keep the egg internal: let it develop there and only then release the offspring. (the fire salamander) The second solution is to take care of the egg (the amazon frog). These two 'improvements' are further elaborated in the reptiles. By improving the reproductive system, many more nutrients can be passed along with the egg. The larval stage can now be eliminated! From the reptiles onwards, both methods are retained and further developed in birds (a large, perfected egg with brood care) and mammals (viviparous with suckling period).

May I invite you to visit the sea or a river in a beautiful, secluded place. Look at the water. Your primal roots are there. You also lived in water for the first nine months. Now dive into the water. Go completely under. Preferably naked. Feel yourself coming home. The water takes away all your worries as it washes around you. When you surface to breathe you may see trees. With their roots, they are in contact with the water. They evaporate it into the air through their leaves. Follow that water vapour into the air. Go under. And again and again... Feel the life, feel the energy. If you are in the sea, let the waves take all your cares away. Feel your ancestors in such a wave... Now come ashore like an amphibian. Try to let the feeling of your birth come over you. In 9 months, you yourself went through that long evolution. Perhaps you feel the urge to jump back into the security, the all-encompassing of the water....

3. Reptiles conquer the land

Vertebrates came ashore later than insects, but they are much more successful. In particular, the choice of an external skeleton in insects appears to be a huge limitation. It is too heavy for large animals to develop. (Think of the well-protective but heavy armour of a knight in medieval times) The size of the internal systems is also limited. Large brains cannot develop within that armour in later evolution.

And there is another thing: the tendency to exaggerate. Specialisation is peculiar to many insects. We already noticed this in the fifth law of evolution, namely socialisation. The social system in bees, ants... is mind-boggling, but their own individuality disappears. This leads to rigidity and paralyses creativity. So we can now formulate a **sixth law**: Too much specialisation leads to rigidity and is a dead end.
Evolution can't move forward anymore and consciousness can't develop further here, as both go together.

But reptiles do not have those limitations at first. From the great range of amphibians, many branches develop. They are not limited in size and conquer the earth. We all know them from fossils. They have become fully terrestrial animals, many of impressive size. Yet they also exaggerate over time. Their external bodies get all the attention. There is no focus to further brain development. Consciousness is not yet large enough.

They also face another major difficulty on land: temperature fluctuations cannot be managed. Their internal temperature is the same as the environment. This becomes fatal to them. With the large meteorite impact along with the turbulent period when India collides with Eurasia and the Himalayas are formed, the earth suddenly cools down. Almost all reptiles die. This is surely already the fifth mass extinction... Only 4 'groups' of smaller animals remain: turtles, crocodiles, lizards and snakes.

4. Birds make the impossible come true

In the meanwhile, small animals that can keep their temperature constant have already developed from the reptiles. We notice two directions. One group that wants to conquer the skies at all costs and one where instinct is not rigidly channelled within one single function: the mammals.

Flying is super difficult. You must not only have wings, but your whole body has to be adapted.

Some examples:
- In the five-finger scheme, only one or two fingers remain to place the flight feathers on
- The bones are hollow because of the weight

- Heart, lungs and digestive system have an extra large capacity to provide the high energy required for flying
- The body temperature is higher than ours to provide the energy required

> We also need large amounts of light fuel in our planes, to have the necessary energy to fly. Now kerosene is used. In the future, we can replace that fuel with green hydrogen.

- To lighten the bird's body, the lungs work with 'air sacs', developed from the respiratory system in snakes
- The head is small and streamlined...etc

It is wonderful how birds have developed! By studying them closely, we have learned to fly ourselves, but their specialisation is too strong. You cannot go back to the basic form to give evolution's search every chance: the sixth law is inexorable!

We can now also extend our first law here. It is very clear that living things become more complicated. You can see this on the outside. But actually, the real development is to be found inside. We cannot observe this objectively. Yet we see that there is a system that reflects the internal consciousness like no other: the nervous system. A more complicated nervous system is an external feature of higher consciousness. From now on, we will take the 'measure and concentration' of this system as the 'external measure' of 'inner consciousness'.

24 May 2007, Nakuru national park, Kenya

Lake Nakuru is home to 1.5 million pink flamingos. On the blue water, they are an unmatchable colour spectacle. We observe their undulating movements very closely. A moving pink sea. Buffaloes and rhinos are real giants. A vulture is a bit more watchable. Pelicans, on the other hand, are extremely graceful. Gazelles are less easy to approach, but you can do it carefully. Zebras in their striped pyjamas look at us. My favourite animal is and remains the impala! They are majestic, graceful animals with beautiful colour bands on their skin. Seeing them so peacefully just beside you...! Some giraffes eat a small tree just like that. What a proud look in that beautiful nature! We come face to face with baboons and monkeys...

May I invite you to find a place in nature where you can watch birds. Let their music sink in. Watch their flight movements. They don't just move their wings up and down. No, it is more like a 'fast rowing motion'. Rowing in the 'water of air...' When you notice this, so much beauty fills you with joy. Perhaps you see a swarm. Look at their fluid movement. Here too, in a swarm, teleportation is proven to be at work among all birds... Let yourself be carried away in that movement. Close your eyes and move gently along in thought. Give yourself wings... and move tender with life....

5. Among mammals, evolution is explosive.

We notice the same thing every time. Strong specialisation is an immediate factor of superiority, but it is irreversible. Specialisation paralyses. Ultra specialisation kills. Throughout evolution there have been catastrophes like this, especially when environmental conditions change. Consider the extinction of giant reptiles. Their external strength and size made them superior. But all development was fixed on this external strength. The internal followed insufficiently. You notice this in their nervous system: they have very small, primitive brains. If the temperature suddenly drops, they are doomed to disappear... But this is necessary to make room for the next evolutionary step that is actually already underway. So instant success is ultimately not success in the long run....

Mammals on the other hand remain adaptable, pliable, individual and social: an aura of freedom. Their brains are larger. Like the birds, they can keep their internal temperature constant and are therefore able to spread throughout the entire earth, across all climatic zones and in all seasons. A range of species evolve from primitive mammals. This can be observed very well by the study of the limbs. Some species develop one finger to walk faster (e.g. the horse). Some walk on their toes to be able to sneak and jump (e.g. the lion). For some, the foreleg becomes a real digging instrument (e.g. the mole). Some have a flight skin stretched between their fingers (e.g. the bat). And if that were not enough: the front legs can also turn into fins (e.g. the seal)... etc. With each of these animals, it is particularly fascinating to see how the basic scheme already present in the amphibians is again beautifully adapted to the environment. The creativity is enormous...! And again, the unity remains here: you keep seeing the basic scheme everywhere.

56 million years ago, there is one group among mammals where specialisation is minimal. No ingenious walking and predatory tools, the five-fingered basal scheme is fearfully guarded, the cranial volume increases... (the measure of consciousness). The primate group (apes, prosimians, great apes and humans) remained free!

Among primates, the great apes (or hominids) have the largest brain capacity, so the greatest consciousness. The 'inergy' rises to a boiling point... There is thought!

Chapter 11

The emergence of thought is a new evolutionary boiling point

The biosphere now spans the entire earth. Between two and five million years ago it seems to be a relaxed phase. Earth is covered with many magnificent species, almost similar to what we know today. The biosphere has become a cooperative whole: an ecosystem. In the tropical and subtropical belt, several species of humanoids evolve. Especially in Africa and India. A quiet abundance reigns In lush forests and endless steppes. But the tranquillity is apparent. The biosphere is gradually evolving. This gradual evolution cannot go on forever. Just as the temperature of water cannot keep rising with the constant addition of heat energy. Suddenly it boils. Here, too, we reach a boiling point, a total threshold crossing as in the origin of life. Either something is alive or it is not. Half-life is impossible. Consciousness has also now reached such a point: not just *'knowing'*, but *'knowing that we know'*. This is **reflection** or **self-awareness!**

All previous consciousness was 'knowing'. We have seen this knowing, this awareness increase. To 'know that you know' is to be able to 'step outside yourself', so to speak, and look at your own life. You look into four-dimensional time-space and know: I am born and I shall also die! This is most typical of thought. Either you can do this, or you can't. You cannot 'half think, half reflect'! The first great ape who could do this was the first human. In whatever branch of the hominids this happened. Perhaps in several branches at once. So you can't be 'half human' either. 78,000 years ago, burial rituals among the first humanoids show us that we have passed this reflection point: they are indeed real human beings! Reflection is sublime, but also immediately the greatest tragedy of being human. We are the only species on earth that lives with the knowledge of its own dying. We suddenly see reality completely differently: in humans, consciousness has become self-consciousness.

> **Bible, Genesis, 3:** Then the woman saw that the tree of knowledge of good and evil had delicious fruits and was pleasing to the eye, and how attractive it was to gain insight from it. So she plucked a fruit and ate it. Then she also gave of some fruit to her husband, who stood by her, and he also ate from it. Now the eyes of both of them opened and they realized that they were naked. So they tied fig leaves together and put them around their hips to cover themselves.

A period on Earth has ended. The biosphere is complete. Thought develops in only a very small part of that immense biosphere. Just as only a very small part of carbon molecules is used for the development of life. Carbon molecules did not become more complicated after that 'momentum' of life. The engine, the carrier of life is perfect. Physically, humanoids are also no more complicated than the other mammals. The size of the brain in the great apes still evolves a bit, (although scientists disagree on how much) but their structure certainly does not. The main branch of evolution, the development of consciousness, is leaving the biosphere and is now concentrated in thought. Like life, thought has only arisen once. Perhaps in several places at the same time, but in one particular period: the 'momentum of thought'. So there is no need to search feverishly for further physical evolution in humans. That evolution is hardly there. These are details. And natural selection between those differences isn't there at all... So if we want to study the main branch of evolution further, it's sufficient to look at thought.

> 'Archaeologists have found the remains of a 78,000-year-old toddler in a Kenyan cave. The child was laid to rest on its side with its legs raised. But what is particularly striking is that the toddler appears to have had a "formal" funeral. And that means researchers have stumbled upon the oldest human-dug grave in Africa here. '

Other changes go along with the birth of thought during that period. Most great apes lived in the tropical zone in the rainforest.

> We already know that the continental drift is Africa slowly splitting in two: the deep rift from the Dead Sea, across the Red Sea, across Somalia to Mozambique.(see chapter 7, 3)

The further splitting off of the humanoids from the large group of Hominidae (common name for humans, great apes, and their common ancestors), probably has to do with the creation of that African rift. Due to the depth of that Rift Valley a different climate appeared on both sides of the gulch. The west had a tropical climate with regular rainfall. The east, towards the Indian Ocean, a climate with alternating wet and dry seasons. This created a much more open landscape in the east, with more difficult living conditions. This gulch, this boundary caused the splitting of the Hominidae so that they evolved as two separate groups. So the humanoids whose fossil remains were found east of that barrier did not in fact come from the forest. The forest itself disappeared from their own environment! In the forest, the 'bent down walking' primates were sheltered from the heat of the tropics. Once out in the open, it was more advantageous not to keep their backs up because the impact of the heat could be too great. Is this a reason to walk upright? Walking upright absorbs 60% less heat. Thus, to the west, chimpanzees and gorillas evaluated further as species that remained adapted to a life in the forest. East of the African rift, however, humans developed a pelvis suitable for upright locomotion. Dentition became more omnivorous and by the shape of the skull we can assume further socialisation. The development of language presupposes a speech centre in the brain.

We probably originated as humans in Africa, recent DNA research confirms. But this does not mean that there cannot be other places. We found so many fossils in East Africa because the natural environment there is particularly well suited for it. In many other places in the world, deposits (sediments) of that particular age are either absent or covered by thick layers of younger rock layers and thus not immediately available for research. Due to the geological action of the many rifts, numerous layers, possibly rich in fossils, were quickly covered. Their later 'uplift' then exposed them again to erosion so that large parts of fossil-rich sediments surfaced and could be discovered. In Europe we also have sediments from the same period, but they are marine deposits in which you obviously do not need to look for fossils of primates.

Or... How environmental changes very likely 'boosted' the emergence of humans. Due to 'difficulties' primates have to adapt to survive (think of Cairns bacteria). Walking upright is one of them: the hands become free. Together with thinking, this is ideal for developing tools. Because the hands are free, the jaw muscles can be relieved. They are no longer needed for grasping and can now become smaller, allowing the brain content in the skull to grow further.

But more importantly, just as cells (the basic entity of life) have come to work together, we see the same in humans (the basic entity of thought).

The Toba catastrophe theory states that the evolution of the human race was significantly influenced by an eruption of the Toba super volcano in Indonesia (Sumatra) around 74,000 years ago. There is no doubt about the death and destruction of the super-eruption itself. According to Stanley H. Ambrose of the University of Illinois, it is possible that the human race Homo sapiens was then decimated to just a few thousand individuals, who, in the harsh volcanic winter that followed, necessarily learned to work better together. In doing so, they made an evolutionary leap that allowed them to displace Homo erectus and Neanderthals, although the latter were more resistant to the cold, and therefore had survived the eruption and winter in larger numbers. This evolutionary 'eye of the needle' would explain the lack of genetic diversity unique to Homo sapiens.

Mahatma Ghandi: 'I am not a visionary, I claim to be a practical idealist. The religion of non-violence is not meant merely for the rishis and saints. It is meant for the common people as well. **Non-violence is the law of our species**, as violence is the law of the brute. The spirit lies dormant in the brute, and he knows no law but that of physical power. The dignity of man requires obedience to a higher law: **the strength of the spirit.'**

The 'driving force' of life are mutations and natural selection. Consciousness 'uses' those mechanisms, as it were. In classical biology, a tiger develops carnivore instincts because 'coincidental' mutations in its ancestors made its teeth or paws better suited for it.

Pierre Teilhard de Chardin: 'The reverse is true: a tiger has a "carnivore consciousness", a "carnivore temperament". This drives the mutations. The inside directs the outside.'

We have recently learned that mutations are quantum-driven. Particles do indeed 'know something'...

To really understand Earth's history, we must try to follow its 'inside': a constant rise in 'inergy', resulting (sometimes in shocks) in higher consciousness.

10 May 2007, Addis Ababa, Ethiopia

In the hustle and bustle of Addis you might forget that Ethiopia and Kenya may be home to the cradle of humanity. We go to the National Museum. Impressive! The oldest 'pre hominid' (precursor of Homo sapiens) has been found in Ethiopia: 4.5 million years old! This makes you silent. Yet the 3.5-million-year-old skeleton of 'Lucy' is most impressive. I know how important this discovery is to get a picture of human evolution and am deeply moved to be able to see this 40% intact skeleton with my own eyes. From here, humans migrated to the Middle East via the Nile Valley. We travelled the same way on our journey.

Briefly summarised:

Ever since the Big Bang, the universe has been changing over time: we call this evolution. Matter, structures, get bigger, more complicated over time. It seems to be an 'urge' that has been present from the origin.

First you notice this evolution in atoms. They get bigger. Then they form molecules. Molecules are larger, more complicated than atoms. It is a 'drive', a constant scanning, trying. Some structures are successful, others are not. The largest, most complicated molecules are formed by the carbon atom. Long chains are formed in a seemingly endless creativity.

Everything is propelled because 'a provisionally non-measurable energy', is constantly being added: the 'inergy'.

A comparison: we evenly add heat to a pot of water on the fire. That heat is not visible to us in the water unless with a thermometer. We notice to our surprise that the water 'suddenly' boils. The addition of that heat energy is now 'suddenly' visible!

Evolution in the universe is a constant rising of 'inergy'. But suddenly we 'see' the 'rise of inergy' in a total external change. We get two such major changes: the transition from non-living to living and the transition to thought. So the emergence of life is not 'sudden', but we *see* it suddenly. It's unmistakable. Everyone, even every animal knows what life is. Either something is alive or it is not. You cannot 'half live'. The same goes for thinking. Either you 'think', or you don't. We can make this distinction as follows: animals 'know', humans 'know that they know'. Man can stand outside himself, as it were, and 'look at himself'. Thinking is reflexive. Again: either you can, or you can't. So you cannot be half-human.

All computer systems on the planet are linked by the internet. They are augmented with artificial intelligence and may approach the capacity of a single human brain computer in the near future. However, we have never detected any form of self-awareness in the system. Why are our 'carbon computers' (our brains) self-aware and our silicon computers zombies?

When we study evolution, we cannot do otherwise than accept that everything has consciousness. Even the non-living. For example, in teleportation, particles 'know' something. The more complicated the structures, the higher the consciousness. In humans, this 'self-awareness' is reflexive.

Evolution is an interplay between mutations in hereditary material and natural selection. We now know that these mutations are not 'blind chance'. They are at least partly driven towards higher consciousness Through the story of the animal kingdom, we can now summarise external evolution in six laws:

Law 1: Animal species become more complex. The development of the nervous system is a measure of the consciousness present.

Law 2: There is great unity in the enormous diversity and creativity.

Law 3: Every revolution is global. A new wrap or 'sphere' is formed. We get successively the hydrosphere, the atmosphere, the lithosphere and the biosphere. They are not separate but form a whole: a global ecosystem.

Law 4: Every crisis gives opportunities. Changing environmental conditions may seem like a disaster but they are not. They give a 'boost' to species that can adapt. Even mass extinction never throws evolution back to a previous stage. No, a catastrophe actually speeds evolution even further.

Law 5: Every species shows the tendency to socialise. Working together is a huge advantage for survival.

Law 6: Excessive external specialisation kills. It seems like an advantage at first, but it makes the species very vulnerable. It paralyses evolution. Sudden changes in the environment are fatal.

In this piece of art, I try to express the emergence of man in Africa. On the lighter-coloured globe, you notice the shape of Africa, where the first human 'erupts'. The hand around the earth is what really matters: consciousness.

Chapter 12

Human evolution walks strange paths

As in the previous evolutionary steps, humans are spreading across the planet. (third law: every revolution is global)

You can divide humans into race (natural) or nation (artificial) but if you give the main direction to thought, this is irrelevant. The general direction of evolution is an unfolding of consciousness. In animals, way of life, instinct,...etc are transmitted to the offspring, but in humans, 'full civilisation' is transmitted via thought: a progressive 'spiritualisation' (Law 1: thinking becomes more complicated).

Just as life has laid a new layer over the earth (the biosphere), a new, 'thinking sphere' is now enveloping the earth. Pierre Teilhard de Chardin calls this the noosphere (nous=mind, spirit)

1. The first people

In the emergence of man, as with all other species, many forms emerged, many try-outs. When we find fossils, man is already well spread over large parts of the earth, using tools, and he talks. The first man is not 'one man', but a crowd. His origin takes thousands of years. It is difficult to find anything of the various 'stems of the fan' of the humans. Most fossils come from the 'fans' itself, as we know already.

7 May 2007, Omorate - Illeret border area Ethiopia - Kenya

Finally, the back of the light truck is packed full of goods and people. We sit and lie mixed up as best we can. There is no road; we drive straight through the vegetation. Branches scrape along your skin. I pull a long thorn out of the back of the boy in front of me. Regularly something falls out of the overloaded car. At the bend another boy flies out of the back of the van... There are also two babies with us in the loading box, clamped in their mother's arms to absorb as many shocks as possible. Others, including us, take turns holding something over the babies' heads against the burning sunlight. Everyone suffers. No one complains. This is Africa too.

For us, it's a unique trip. The majestic nature in the world's largest rift valley. But not only that. We will ride from village to village as ordinary passengers, bearing silent witness to tribal life as it may have existed in the Stone Age....

It cannot be described. So overwhelming. Children walk naked and are absorbed into that colourful nature. The graceful, also almost naked bodies of young men and women were created by the 'Sculptor', even greater than the most famous sculptor Rodin. The bodies of older men and women are also making me quiet. I look at an older woman and see a sculpture from the Musée Rodin in Paris (she who was the helmet-maker's beautiful wife) before me. Very skinny. She has had many children. Her breasts and belly show this life's work. In our western culture, we call this a sagging, worn-out body and you try to camouflage it a bit. Here, you can be proud of such a body, and the woman also radiates this. I think she's very handsome. You could cherish her wrinkled face in your two hands, because this body also shows you how hard life is here. The young woman next to her has not yet had any children. She is a real beauty. The taut skin around the perfect body shape radiates youth and vitality. The 'Master Sculptor'....

Then Lake Turkana looms, the cradle of humanity. (see photo 6 on www.scienceandspirituality.be)

My heart jubilates with joy and I am moved. Clouds pack together. Everyone has seen it coming, the daily portion in the rainy season. It's raining cats and dogs. We huddle even closer together under a canvas, but everything is instantly soaking wet. The road becomes a slide in no time and just

before the border with Kenya we are irrevocably stuck in the mud. In the pouring rain, with a kilo of mud on each foot: digging out, branches under the wheels, pushing... At 6 pm we arrive in Illeret, the first village in Kenya.
The next day, under the steel-blue sky, I dive into the salty Lake Turkana. I feel the intensity of the water. You are intoxicated by all those colours. The cradle of humanity... Breathtaking.

In the beginning, you may still have doubts. It is difficult to infer the way of life, and even much more difficult, the state of consciousness, from a small part of a skull. But with the Neanderthal branch, it is certain. This is a real human being. (See diagram) We find many fossils and see burial rituals. All human races outside Africa have DNA from the Neanderthals. Also our human species, Homo sapiens.

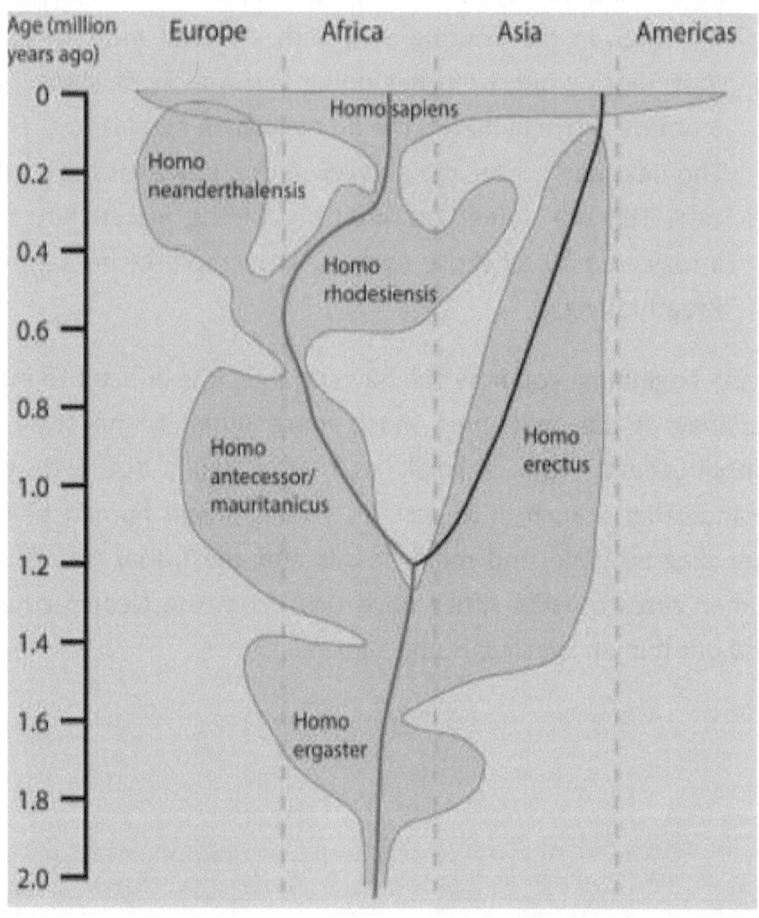

One of the evolutionary schemes of man until 2 million years ago (Homo rhodesiensis is the same as Homo heidelbergensis)

2. Homo sapiens

12 July 1997: Christine and I are camping in the Ariège region, at the foot of the French Pyrenees:

Christine: *I would like to go to the Niaux cave. It's only 7 km from here. The cave is famous for its cave paintings.*

 Me*: Pfffff... you have to book by phone and a guide must accompany you. Blah blah blah, to see some indistinct lines, where you then have to imagine an animal or something.*

Christine: *Yes, but I'm going to call anyway. If you don't want to come then I'll go alone.*

Me: *Holala, the strong sex. Well, shall we go then?*

We can get an appointment two days later. With a guide, we enter the 'salon noir'. My mouth falls open. These paintings, made with black, flowing lines and more than 12,000 years old, depict large mammals from prehistoric fauna such as bison, horses, deer and ibexes. The lines show exceptional gracefulness. The beauty moves me deeply. I follow the artful lines with my eyes and feel the connection. This is not just created. You feel the intuition. This Cro-Magnon man, one of the first representatives of Homo sapiens is a real human being: creativity and playfulness are fully present.

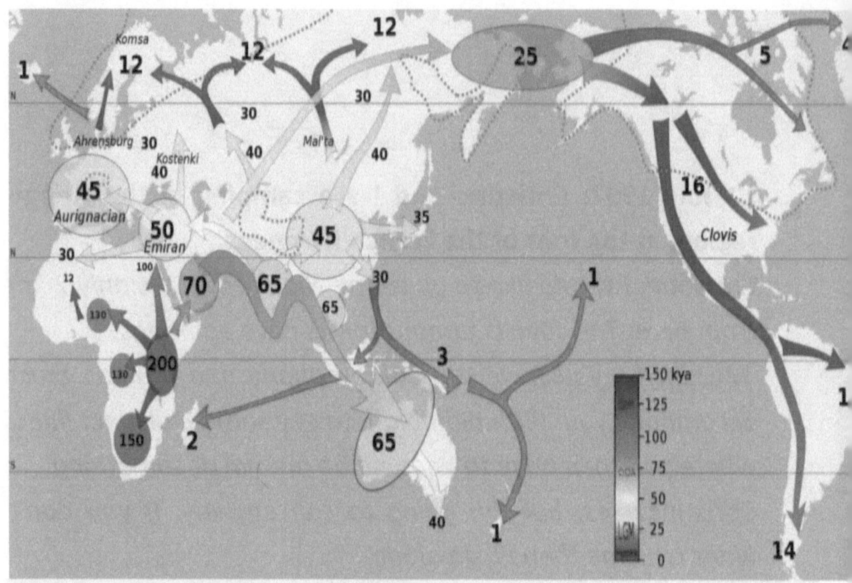

This map shows the 'possible' spread of the different human tribes. The numbers indicate how many years
(X 1,000) this is ago.

So Homo sapiens almost certainly originated in Africa. Playfulness, art, imagination, joy of creation were already present. From then on, humans barely evolved physically. The socialisation we already noticed in higher animal species is constantly getting stronger.

The spread dominates the whole earth as you can see on the map above, but this dispersal creates groups that develop a lot of differences in ways of life depending on the circumstances. These become traditions: the collective memory emerges. Real civilisations are born!

About 11,000 years ago we see the same trend everywhere: the transition from a society of itinerant hunter-gatherers, to an agricultural society, again perhaps necessary because of a changing climate. This is called the 'Neolithic revolution'.

According to current insights, people established in permanent settlements in about 11,000 BC, in the Fertile Crescent (from the Nile to Mesopotamia). These 'villages' slowly grew larger and also became more and more secure. Eventually, they evolved into city-states. In the beginning, the inhabitants still gathered wild crops for their livelihood. They started protecting the fields with those wild crops from wild animals. Later, much more attention was paid to these fields. Agriculture may have received a boost in the early Neolithic due to a climatic change: a cold period that made the climate in southwest Asia much drier. By weeding and planting seeds obtained from elsewhere, yields improved. According to new findings, experiments on breeding grain varieties were already being carried out around 20,000 BC. Later on, cattle breeding also began. Until then, mainly wild animals had been hunted. As herds of wild animals gradually began to disappear, the domestication of sheep, goats, cattle and pigs began. Around 6200 BC, global temperatures dropped briefly and suddenly (8k2 event). This accelerated that development.

The 'human mind' is now the leader of those developments. No longer the 'body'. In animals, natural selection is one of the main mechanisms. Not anymore. With the humans, civilisations intertwine. Even in wars and conquests, there is assimilation. Think of the Jews in Canaan. Or the Celts, ancient Teutons with the Romans in Gaul. There is also trade. In the beginning, there is little contact between the Americas and the rest of the world. This changes in the 16th century.

According to British researchers, the colonisation of both Americas by Europeans was one of the causes of the so-called Little Ice Age, the period between roughly 1450 and 1850, when the Earth's average temperature was slightly lower than before and after. The Little Ice Age caused severe winters in Europe, known from Bruegel's paintings. In America, 55 million original inhabitants died from war, forced labour, economic malaise and especially diseases brought by Europeans. As a result 56 million hectares of farmland turned into wasteland (the area of France). The researchers calculated that those new wild trees and plants absorbed enough CO_2 to lower the global temperatures by one or two tenths of a degree (this is the reverse of global warming now). They took samples of ice at the South Pole, ice that formed during that Little Ice Age. Those samples contained air bubbles. Analysis of the air bubbles in that ice showed that there was indeed less CO_2 in the air during that period than before and after. The disappearance of farmland in North and South America was only one of the causes of the temperature drop. Changes in sea currents, volcanic eruptions and reduced solar activity also played a role.

3. The great world civilisations

From the 16de century, the entire earth was connected. This often happened with many growing pains. It is the beginning of a coherent whole around the earth. Five focal points emerge, each with their strengths and weaknesses.

1. The European (including Russia) culture, with those of North and South America derived from it (mixed with the original Indian culture), plus Australia and New Zealand (mixed with the Aboriginal culture, although little of that remains).

An enormous freedom has developed in European culture after many deep and painful upheavals. A phenomenal scientific knowledge has changed our view of everything. It led to the modern inventions we use today: cars, aeroplanes, telecommunications... That scientific knowledge has been spread all over the world and is now everywhere. Other cultures are rapidly adopting it.

European culture has been dominant over the past hundreds of years and has contributed to the development of the planet like no other. But there is also a downside: the European nations have exploited many peoples and plundered their countries. That looting is still going on. They also almost destroyed themselves in two major conflicts in the past century...The planet has been largely damaged by that way of development.

Therefore Europeans are in debt to all other peoples and also the planet....

There is more. Europeans turned away from the internal. Due to the emphasis on material development, the spiritual was largely lost. We know from the sixth law of evolution that this is a wrong track. Think of the large reptiles. Contact with the whole has also been lost. We are part of the global ecosystem but have forgotten that. (Third Law) The fifth law (socialisation) is also going wrong: material affluence and an emphasis on economic growth have severely damaged the social fabric. For many Europeans, these deficits put pressure on the internal. Intuitively people sense that something is wrong in the current development.

2. The Indian culture: In India, the emphasis does lie on developing the internal. Freedom here, as in Europe, is little curtailed except by religious laws. (Think of the caste system). You can feel the energy crackle into people... if they stay alive. Until a few decades ago, poverty was distressing for a part of the population. Due to the overemphasis on spirituality, the connection with reality was too small. We know from the third law that our bodies are part of the ecosystem: if you can't absorb food, you can forget about everything else too. This is changing very quickly. By following the European development model, life has improved a lot for large population groups. Life in the big cities has undergone a metamorphosis, even for the poorest. But because of this rapid development, as with us in the beginning, you get an environmental disaster. Air and water pollution take the form of a true epidemic.

3. The Chinese culture is built on a very old tradition with great spirituality. Here, rigidity is the culprit. Since ancient times. Communism has made this even more intense. We already know that too rigid socialisation leads to a system that kills freedom and creativity (think of an ant colony). This became an unmitigated disaster under Mao. This system has been abandoned, economically anyway. Creativity is possible again in the economy, in many other areas it remains difficult. Again, the European development model has been adopted with all the environmental problems involved.

4. The Polynesian culture around the South Pacific radiates an oasis of calm.

5. The culture in the Nile and Mesopotamia region, along with the many African cultures: here, due to various circumstances, development fell far behind. This gives the advantage that the link with nature was preserved as on no other continent.

This overview is very succinct and absolutely detracts from the wonderful diversity and creativity of human culture ...

How do we have to move forward now? Critical points enough! But stagnation? If you don't see the noögenesis, it seems hopeless...

Life does not keep turning its circles. We cannot go back to the past. The spirit propels on...

Either we believe in a meaningless, immense universe with tiny human beings that happened to originate on an earth that is now in danger of going crazy, or we look at our evolution in the past. Our own history has taught us that the two great moments (emergence of life and thought) cannot come back, but neither can life and thought disappear! Despite major catastrophes. And there have been more than enough of those! If you study the proportion of past catastrophes, you know that the climate change coming our way is not exceptional. It is for the first time however that we have at least partly caused this change ourselves.

The big changes of the last decades, think climate, have been happening for a while. What we are experiencing now is just the beginning. We would prefer everything to remain the same, but we know from the fourth law of evolution that changes have always been there and that they drive evolution forward... *'Unfolding' of consciousness.*

It's now time to look at those evolutionary laws in the future! We are at a crossroads. A new era is beginning. And we get to participate in this era...! We get to join the *awakening*! Fantastic... Because we ourselves are the evolution!

in this piece of art, I try to express that the earth is carried by 'self consciousness'.

25 April 2007, Abri, northern Sudan (see photo 7 on www.scienceandspirituality.be)

During one of the last bus stops, we witness a heart breaking scene. A dozen women take their seats on our bus. They may be leaving for a very long time. Heart breaking sobbing. Half the neighbourhood is gathered. As we drive away, the sobbing turns into heartrending crying of grief. The typical high-pitched guttural sound with rattling tongue is emitted. Panic! An inferno! How bad. With screeching tyres we dash away and we also sympathise a little. We almost dare not look up at all this human suffering... I hide behind my chair a bit.

But don't I hear laughter there? Unbelievably, in a few minutes the tears have dried and the atmosphere is more than exuberant: there is laughter, screeching, singing, roaring. Much, much louder than a bus of elated schoolchildren returning from the annual school trip. You don't understand what they shout at the men, but I would certainly call the glances back and forth lascivious!

This goes on and on. Until I want to take a picture of the little boy falling asleep on Christine's lap. The mother straightens up. 'It's not allowed!' Hup, fun done. A loud discussion erupts with pros and cons. But the mom (2 X Christine's volume and not a kitten to be handled without gloves!) doesn't want it. For us, no point. Discussion closed. The singing, roaring, clapping, dancing... continues. Lovely such a bus!

'Crazy mum' has a large round flat basket in woven straw with her luggage. A rather clumsy thing on such a crammed bus. She tries to force the thing on everyone, which is refused with loud murmurs by the other passengers. It lands next to the woman just in front of me. But she slowly slides the round thing in my direction!

I regularly push him back with my foot. What are those matrons thinking? Suddenly I see an electrical conduit about 5 cm from the ceiling. The straw thing might just fit in between. I grab the straw soup dish and push it between the tube and the ceiling. The ideal place. No one is bothered by it now! But an unimaginable uproar erupts. I am congratulated, patted on the back, everyone wants to see me as if I were the winner of the last Nobel Prize. Especially the men, but also the women burst out laughing. What an unexpected solution! (Because, of course, everyone was passing the buck and following with suspense who would lose the game...)

After 10 hours of driving, we arrive in Abri around midnight.

Look at a satellite photo of the Earth. Our beautiful blue planet. With such diversity. Look at the continents. Look at Africa and think about the story of the bus. How intensely people live here. How exuberantly. Are you also living exuberantly? Or could it be a bit more? Then look at our atmosphere. It consists of about 20 per cent oxygen. If this were a few percent more, everything would be on fire. We would not survive this...A miracle.

Water expands when it solidifies. An exception in physics. This is why icebergs float. If icebergs didn't float, (all other solids sink in their own liquid) all those blue seas you see in the picture would freeze over. All the water would form one block of ice, down to the bottom. All the rivers, lakes. We would never have come into existence... Two 'coincidences'? No. Mother Earth takes care of us: Indians, Africans know it: the Pachamama . Now look at Europe. At the beautiful shape. A hand. Africa's shape resembles a heart. Close your eyes and let that African zest for life flow through you. Make the connection with Europe.... Put your hand on your heart and feel gratitude for the miracle of the Pachamama.

Chapter 13

The laws of evolution show us the way to a wonderful future for earth and man. Confluence of thought

1. Technical capabilities connect us externally

In 1991, British **Tim Berners-Lee revolutionised** the world by creating the world wide web (www). Not only could this allow files to be sent, but information could also be stored in the network itself and viewed via a web browser. On 23 August 1991, the world wide web was opened to everyone. From then on, any individual could theoretically use the network. A factoid in the news on 24 August 1991... A new strand in the nervous system of the noosphere.

We recognise very well the ordinary mechanisms of evolution among the first humanoids. These start with searching, probing... until one of those twigs becomes a mega-success:

Homo sapiens. The 'fan structure' is recognisable, with also all features such as a global spread. Environmental adaptations (think skin colour) and mutations within the group create differences: the different human races and peoples on our earth.

But there is a big difference with evolution in plants and animals: the different 'rays' of the group that emerge from the 'fan structure' of Homo sapiens are no longer separated from each other. The human fan structure, the human 'screen', expands as a *whole* because all human races can still reproduce with each other. Through transport and means of communication in our modern world, we meet frequently. More and more, offspring are born from two cultures. The human fan structure does not form separate 'new stems' as in a normal biological evolutionary process. The 'fan structure' remains an entity!

> **Josephine Baker:** 'There is only one race, namely the human race.'

That entity is still hesitating, but will grow stronger in the future. And the 'entity' are getting bigger:

The nation states

Industrial development, war, power deployment... ensure the creation of European nation-states. Nationalism wants us to believe that this is something natural. Or not. It is not difficult to show that the concept of 'country' and 'people' just doesn't make sense. The confluence of multiple population groups always causes friction. In the past and... also now.

> The mass emigration of the Flemish people began with the economic crisis in the mid-19th century, which drove unemployed workers and poor small farmers away from their region. While agriculture and the textile industry were hit hard in Flanders, industry began to flourish in Wallonia, where they were short of hands. The population in the centres with coal mines and steel factories grew rapidly and much more strongly than, for example, in Antwerp, at that time the strongest growth centre in Flanders. Louis de Raet gives figures for the Walloon industrial towns between 1864 and 1890: in Charleroi, Walloons made up only 34.35% of the population, in Verviers 54.72%, in Mons 55.41%, in Liège 56.43%, in Seraing 59.32%, in Jumet 61.45%, in Gilly 65.18% and in Tournai 66.27%. The rest are immigrant Flemings.

Even then, there was a lot of friction with the original Walloon population.

Europe

This evolution to bigger units does not stop within nation-states, but continues. First economically.

> **The agreement of 20 June 1946**
>
> Migration of 50,000 Italian workers to Belgium in exchange for the annual sale of 2-3 million tonnes of coal to Italy. They often did the heavy work in our mines. The Marcinelle mining disaster of 8 August 1956 took the lives of 262 people, including 136 Italians. That disaster revealed that working conditions in the mine were appalling ...

Europe is a test laboratory of peaceful amalgamation. By concluding treaties, far-reaching cooperation has emerged. A unique experiment in the world.

> **1946 Winston Churchill**: *'We must build a kind of United States of Europe'*
>
> He urged Europeans to turn their backs on the horrors of the past and look to the future. He declared that Europe could not afford to continue in an atmosphere of hatred and revenge springing from the injuries of the past. For Churchill, the first step in recreating the 'European family' of justice, mercy and freedom.

> **9 May 1950 Robert Schuman** launches a proposal: France, Germany, and possibly other European countries, could manage their steel industry together, as if there were no borders anymore.

Jean Monnet and Konrad Adenauer saw France and West Germany return to that fatal rivalry and bidding in 1950, just as they did after World War I. Especially around their steel and thus weapons industry. This had to stop. So the trio broke the old dynamic of rivalry, envy and war between the continent's two most sworn enemies, and after the creation of the ECSC began the adventure of the European Union.

The Erasmus programme for the academic year 2018-2019 had a record number of more than 6,000 Flemish higher education students. They follow part of their studies or internships in another European country. That was almost 2,800 more than a decade earlier.

India

Mahatma Gandhi became India's religious and political leader. He wanted his country to become independent. Not by taking up arms but by 'non-violent resistance': protest marches, hunger strikes and an economic boycott of British goods. That is why he also called on his followers to take up spinning, weaving and making clothes themselves. Not only so that poor peasants had an additional means of livelihood, but also to forge a bond between his various followers, including Muslims and Hindus. Textiles were a British import product. By making their own clothes, Indians became less dependent.

We mark that some people are visionary. They have the inner strength to hold on to their vision completely against the grain. (Even if that means half a life in prison as in the case of Nelson Mandela, for example.)

Not only Europe and India but a number of other areas come closer to unity. We can't discuss them all here...

If that unity is obtained through war and conflict as in the civil war of the United States, the fault lines remain because that unity is insufficiently supported internally. The polarization in present-day American society partly originates there.

The world

Even reprehensible practices such as slave trade, exploitation through neoliberalism resulting in the huge disparity between rich and poor in the world (resulting in the flood of refugees...) ensure that the formation of that unity, that noosphere, with many growing pains accelerates across the world!

> **Tagore:** Suffering is great, but man is greater than suffering

> In the 17th and 18th centuries, the triangular trade was at its peak and large numbers of slaves were bought by mainly Portuguese, English, but also Spanish and Dutch traders on the coast of West Africa and sold in the Americas. The current estimate is that 12 million slaves were transported from Africa to the Americas.

The great breakthrough of neoliberalism came in the 1980s with politicians Ronald Reagan (US) and Margaret Thatcher (UK). 'The government is not the solution to our problems, government is the problem'. The 'invisible hand' of the market, through the 'ingenious' interplay of supply and demand, would henceforth solve all social and economic problems. Everything that disturbs the 'natural' market forces must give way: public services, taxes for the rich, trade unions, regulations and, in fact, the government as a whole. Inequality is no longer an ailment but a blessing, a necessity for wealth creation. Neoliberalism was accepted by just about every political movement in the 1990s. It brought a very rapid development in countries such as China and India. That 'development boost' is a blessing for millions of people in poverty, but there are side effects:

1. The economy has become global.
2. Pollution is a global problem
3. Immense inequality is created, resulting in large refugee flows.

The human range is melting together all over the globe. We are meeting each other. The economy is already fully global. The rest will follow. You cannot work against the drive of the laws of evolution... An unlimited mutual fertilisation. The whole earth is covered in one membrane.

We are getting globalisation on all levels. Peoples have become so interdependent that they can only grow by developing all together. There is no point in trying to maintain old habits. We cannot solve international conflicts like we used to. A first step is to conclude treaties, make agreements.

Pierre Teilhard de Chardin, 10 December 1948
'The Universal Declaration of Human Rights is the visible birth of the noosphere... My heart rejoices!'

Saturday 12 December 2015 is a historic turning point
After years of arduous negotiations, 195 countries signed an ambitious and legally binding climate agreement towards a climate-neutral future at the end of the Paris climate conference. This agreement is universal and fair, because for the first time a treaty text has been adopted that requires efforts from all parties and thus eliminates the old dichotomy between developed countries (which until now were the only ones with the obligation to reduce their emissions), developing and emerging countries (which until now had no such obligation). The developed countries must finance that turnaround in the poorer countries. In Paris we have seen many revolutions over the past centuries, but today the most beautiful and peaceful one is taking place: the climate change revolution.
Specifically, this means a reduction in greenhouse gas emissions for European Union countries by 80-95% in 2050 (compared to 1990). This has been adjusted in the 'green deal' to 100% because Europe wants to play a pioneering role.

2. The real change is internal

So, externally, we see unity emerging. But, everything is driven by the inside. The 'inergy' rises... and pushes... towards a power concentration of consciousness. Especially through the mind, the spirit. In thinking we meet: we become one humanity. The formation of one thinking and feeling system: the noosphere. We are in crisis because non-integrated forces are erupting. Man does not know what to do with the power he himself unleashed... If we want to keep our old 'hovels', this will explode in our faces. If only we can open our eyes... We are entering a totally new realm of inner 'totalisation' of the world: the building of a 'spirit of the earth'. As in our personal lives, it is by trial and error. Every transition takes 'inergy'. You can't see the forest for the trees... Within the time span of one generation, seemingly not much happens.

> You have to add a lot of heat energy to convert an entire pot of water into water vapour. You only add heat energy, and nothing changes about the temperature. The pot stays at 100°C. What's the point? But... we hadn't noticed the vapour: a revolution!

It is normal that, in the midst of this transition, discouragement lurks around the corner: humans will never become unified... There will always be war... We cannot save the earth and the climate... The story repeats itself... etc. Discouragement is the biggest pitfall.

Individualism is another trap. It is positive that we can develop our individuality. It is a life purpose for every human being. But if we see our personal development as separate from the whole, not at the service of that whole, we will not become happy. We so sense that this does not correspond to the 2nd law: evolution is a drive towards unity in diversity. Nor with the 3th law: We globally form a biosphere and a noosphere. The 5th law tells us that socialisation is indispensable for further evolution. So individualism stands in the way of our own growth of consciousness. And we get that message from our 'inside' via a sense of restlessness, uneasiness, melancholy. The number of depressions, suicides... has never been higher in the Western world. Our 'inner self' cries out for change, as the 'inergy' rises and finds no rest in a further ascent of our consciousness.

Out of that sense of unease or because of the inequality in society we see an escape into racism and nationalism. They give a false 'good feeling' because there is connection with other 'like-minded' people here. So the 5th law (socialisation) is followed here. But the 2nd and the 3rd law show: it is at the expense of others.
Look to the world and surely to Europe what nationalism can lead to... So it also stands in the way of our own development of consciousness. A disaster for humanity...

Jalal ad-Din Rumi: 'Why do you stay in the prison of your own self, when the door is so wide open?'

We search in all sorts of directions. Trying and trying...

Because we as human beings consist of matter, we are constantly inclined to follow 'external changes'. This or that law or rule will solve it.

Karl Marx describes the ideal society in a wonderful way. After reading his work, I also became a convinced Marxist for several years! Later, I understood that most external revolutions are insufficiently supported from within. If the emphasis is entirely on the system, they are doomed to get bogged down in lack of freedom. There is no connection with the 'inside'. It becomes an 'empty' system as in an anthill or bee colony.

Therefore, even when alliances arise from 'internal' consciousness, as was certainly the case with the founding of India, not every person has that feeling yet. It's an evolutionary process.

30 January 1948, New Dehli

Mahatma Gandhi could not prevent the conflict between Islam and Hindu communities leading to civil war and the secession of Pakistan and present-day Bangladesh. A fanatical Hindu shot Gandhi because he thought he was too loyal to the Muslims. Gandhi died on the spot. According to bystanders, his last words were: 'Hai Ram' (O God).

20 April 1972, Brugge, Belgium, Onze-Lieve-Vrouwecollege
I am a class teacher in the second year of a secondary school and in April I know that three of my students are not doing well. If it continues like this they will not pass. I decide to do something. I myself am not at home in all subjects but I give them the opportunity to learn together on every Saturday morning with the three brightest students in my class who can then give them expert tuition. One pupil drops out, but the other two come every Saturday morning. They achieve a spectacularly good result for their final term and pass without any problem. This gives me great satisfaction. Next school year, I no longer teach those two students, but follow their results. They are no good at all and fail in the next year. The pupil who dropped out does succeed in his third year of technical education. A hard lesson for me. If a decision does not come from the 'inside' of that pupil, for example they do it for me, it makes no sense.

8 November 2006 Varanasi, India
I note in my diary: 'We walk towards the city', vendors and rickshaw drivers evading us, as always. A bicycle rickshaw driver continues to follow us.
- *I want to take you around for an hour for 10 rupees ($0.1).*

- Sorry, we just want to walk at our leisure, and don't need a rickshaw right now. By the way, if you drive an hour for us, you should not do so for 10 rupees!

Yet the man continues to haunt us...
We turn into a tiny street where the cycle rickshaw can hardly pass. Added bonus: There is a beer shop in that street! We buy a bottle of beer and settle on the edge of the pavement.
But unbelievably, after a few minutes the man is standing in front of us again:
- Where do you want to go, you've already walked such a long way?
- It's not far, just to an internet café, we like to walk...
Want a sip of beer too?
- No, I never drink beer because it's way too expensive for me.
Ashamed, I think our beer costs 65 rupees, and the man is chasing us for 10 rupees. Yet, it is so hard to know what to do... We tell him:
- Join us and have a drink. You may then lead us to the internet café later.
- You may not understand this. I am poor, have 3 small children and am struggling. I have to pay a 'permit' for the rickshaw. Moreover, I am not the owner of the rickshaw. I rent it every day for 50 rupees from my boss because I cannot get the money together to buy one myself. So my first customers are for him every day... The house, where

my family stays, costs 1000 rupees ($10) every month, the electricity 300. My name is Hira. I cannot read or write.

- Namasté. Christine and Johan. We have four children aged between 22 and 27. How old are your children?

- 6, 4 and 1 years. I myself am as old as your eldest son, 27. How old are you?

- 50 and 51

- You are 'mum and dad' to me.

- What does a new rickshaw actually cost?

- 8,000 rupees

- And a second-hand one?

- 4,500

During the drive, we thought maybe we could do something for Hira...

A little math. We come back in 3 months, 50 rupees rent money X 90 days = 4,500 rupees ($90). We could lend this amount to him, just enough for a second-hand rickshaw and in 90 days he would save 4,500 rupees in rent money. For us, a small amount...

He drops us off at the internet cafe.

- I'll wait for you, no matter how long it takes. Then I'll take you back. Please.

- No, we don't want that. Don't wait. Maybe we can help you buy your own rickshaw so you become your own boss.

- This would be fantastic for me. Tomorrow I will introduce you to my family.

- OK, come tomorrow at 8 am.

9 November 2006, Varanasi, India (next day)

We leave around 8 o'clock. We turn into the Muslim quarter, smaller and smaller streets, until the rickshaw is parked.

- I am from Bengal, not far from Calcutta and I am Muslim. The house we're renting isn't really that good, but you are welcome

Through a door, we enter a kind of wasteland, teeming with children among the many slum dwellings. It's a bit of a scare. We had expected a house, or at least some rooms.

We enter. The house is one room measuring 3 x 4 metres. Although, room...

Bamboo was used to make a shelter against a wall. Not completely waterproof. The other three walls consist of discarded burlap bags. The floor is earth.

A mat is rolled out for the high visit. We take our seats and are offered tea.

The first moment you don't know where to look. You are so ashamed of your own wealth...

But, if you are a bit more at ease, you see that everything here is spick and span. The little they have has its place. The hovel on the outside is beautiful on the inside. His wife could easily win the Miss Belgium and Miss Belgian Beauty Contest together. The children look very neat. Can't understand how that is possible. They have a real home here and look happy. Which is not to say that minimum needs are met here. Such conditions are inhuman to us. Yet here again you see the enormous creativity of a human being to build 'a piece of happiness' with so little. No despair here, but hope. We have learnt this many times on this journey: everything is much more hopeful and positive than you see on a photo...

It is terrible for Hira, not to have security of existence. Having to look for tomorrow's food. 200 rupees ($2) every day is a minimum.
- A big bag of rice is cheaper per kg, but we cannot buy this in one go. The gas bottle is empty. No money for a new one, we gather wood for cooking... We'll get by.
Meanwhile, I see that Hira's family has to share their 'room' with a family of mice, whose burrow exits into the hut just next to me.
What I find most terrible is the rent: 1,000 rupees a month, for something like that! And then the rent for that rickshaw! 1,500 a month. Electricity 300. Others still get rich on the sweat of such people.

We decide to give them 500 rupees to buy a big bag of rice, a new gas cylinder, and we lend them 4,500 rupees to buy a second-hand rickshaw. This amount must be refunded when we return in early February. Of course, we can also give this. But this way it's not a handout, just a small support that will enable them to build a slightly better situation on their own.

We say goodbye to the family. Hira leads us around the Muslim quarter where many houses have looms for silk.

Manual work is a Muslim speciality. The selling is done by Hindus. We end up also at the sales department as usual. And... Hira will also get his percentage.

We are carried back and agree to meet again in three months. Hira wants us to join his family for dinner then. We gladly agree and promise to have a picture of his family printed in Belgium. (see photos 8 and 9 on www.scienceandspirituality.be)

9 February 2007, Varanasi, India (3 months later)
We saw Hira briefly, yesterday. He doesn't have the money. Actually, we'd like to give him the 4,500 rupees ($50), yet something is wringing. He is already waiting for us, and without thinking, it can't resist saying:
- I don't want you to take us around everywhere for several days for free. We're happy to pay you for that, but you also have to keep your promise. Can you repay the borrowed 4,500 rupees?
Hira looks at me deeply unhappy.
- I don't have it. I can't pay it back today. I had unexpected expenses because my mom needed an surgery operation. I paid part of that and also my train ticket to travel to Calcutta. You see. All my family lives there, but because they abolished all bicycle rickshaws in Calcutta (a 'good' measure because this is way too hard work for people), I came to Varanasi. I just can't do anything else.
- We'll talk about it later, but you made a promise...

The day starts a little tense, but the friction ebbs away as we drive on. We drive to some more distant Buddhist temples and ashrams (where a surprising number Westerners stay). All sacred places, but it doesn't tell us much.

When we arrive at his home, Hira is already very excited. 'My wife has made chapati (a kind of flat bread) for you. You are my friends and guests today'.
The whole neighbourhood is expecting us. After extensive introductory formalities, we enter the house. Still a hovel. Burlap bags, some with holes, form the walls. But there is TV now. *'4100 rupees,'* Hira tells us excitedly. *'The children are everything to me and a television is just what they need. 'My friend lent me 4000 rupees, but I had to pay back 4400'.*
'Hum, friend' I think to myself, just the amount we borrowed. And also a big, new clock on the wall. *'We need to know what time it is, don't we?'* You notice from the children that they are much more lavish with the rice than three months ago.

Hira's family is decked out as beautifully as it can be. They exude an incredible vitality.
Dinner is ready: chapati with rice and chicken. Chicken is a great luxury for them. When they want to get beer, we refuse. The food is very tasty, and we are incredibly welcome. I doubt I'll bring up the refund again. But especially that TV that is quite loudly broadcasting the

most silly quiz or so, keeps bothering me. Nobody watches it.

We talk, and it's great fun, but after a while I ask Hira:

- *What about your promise?*

- *It will be fine, but I actually used the money for my mother. (shows the train tickets to Calcutta). I just need to go away for a while now.*

Hira stays away for quite some time, I go in search of him.

- *I was able to strike a good deal with my friend. You may choose for 4,500 rps in his silkshop, and then I will have time to pay it back to him.*

(again handy from that 'friend')

- *But we don't want silk at all.*

- *I'll sort it out.*

After a few hours, we say goodbye. Hira leads us back. On parting:

- *I will come tomorrow to say goodbye, and bring the money.*

But we can't resist asking:

- *How do you get it?*

At first we don't understand it very well, but then it comes out:

- *I can pawn my rickshaw, and work for my old boss again with a borrowed rickshaw. Once I get the money back, I can buy back my rickshaw.*

(You can't imagine what exorbitant interests he has to add)

- *We don't want you to sell your rickshaw.*

- I can only offer you the TV then. He's about worth this. You can have it.

- No, we don't want that.

- I want to keep my promise. I'll manage. Will you run out of money then? asks Hira honestly.

We explain to him that it's not about the money, but about something he promised, and that it is important to put something aside every day to pay back, or to improve the house or something. We talk for a long time, and see that he now fully understands. We make him a proposal:

-We trust you, put aside 30 rupees every day, and when you have the amount in full, transfer it to us. We want to help you further with your children's school, but first you must keep your promise. We don't want to be driven around for free either. We will pay 500 rupees for those 2 days. So you have to save only 4000 rupees.

- I am immensely happy. I will work hard, and have 4500 rupees transferred to you. I don't want money for those days. But now I still want to take you to the cremation on the Ganges River.

We look at the photos on the laptop with him and let him choose some, to print in the photoshop, which doesn't work. He talks endlessly, we almost drive into a car as he looks back.

Everywhere you have to fend Hiras who want to get a piece of the pie... beggars, the boat's oarsman, children selling flowers, begging... Thousands and thousands of Hiras... this evening alone. You can't give them all money, and even if you could, nothing may have been solved. What does solving mean? Perhaps there would be a lot more TVs on in India?

You don't know what to do. Should we teach Hira to save? At the end of the day, he is a happy man. And when those children go to such a school?

Who are we to say what should be? Are we so much happier in a good home? Many questions, few answers. And, you certainly shouldn't have the pretention to come here and say what they have to do, because those people may be much happier in their lives than many Belgians. We stare blindly at their bad house or... their purchase of a TV for their children on credit? But when you look at the face of those Bengali people. Yes, man. They are alive. Where are we?? We don't know anything. Everything has so many sides.

20 November 2016, Varanasi (9 years later)
This time, I am here alone. It has been 9 years since I was in this beautiful city and we met Hira. And of course, we never got back the $50 from Hira. The city has changed. You don't see that abject poverty anymore. You are no longer constantly accosted. The rubbish is now collected, which gives a much neater street scene. There is reasonably good healthcare. Traffic and air pollution have increased

dramatically, though. Unbearable. I look for Hira again and bring a nice chicken. The photos from 2006 have also been printed. The reunion is most cordial. We talk endlessly. Also how he lost his eldest son in a car accident...He often feels down. Then drink and drugs lurk around the corner. His wife has a hard time with that too....

February 25, 2019 Varanasi (3 years later)
I am visiting my friend Hira again and bring a chicken and a bag of rice. *'Allah has given us another child to make up for the misfortune of my eldest son. And my 13-year-old daughter has been married off! Allah will give me grandchildren next year!'* Hira is a happy man again. But their cottage, again on another wasteland, looks shabby and dilapidated. I can't believe they live there now. The deep wrinkles in his wife's face show that their life is tough. Hira is not surfing the wave of spectacular life improvement in India. He has abilities, however. As an illiterate, he speaks perfect English. I don't understand...

With my students, the decision was not sufficiently internalised. With Hira, it wasn't either. It is a slow process.

This is perhaps also the reason why the outcome of many wonderful development or education projects is disappointing...

Even revolutions do not change anything immediately if they are not carried internally: the French Revolution rightly wanted to do away with the power of the French king. Eleven years later, Napoleon crowned himself...

emperor! The communist revolution in Russia delivered Stalin... Only gradually could the ideals of the French revolution spread across Europe and bear fruit.

We know from evolution that consciousness, the inside is the most important thing, but often forget that. If that is not present, it is only external changes that often lead to nothing.

Jalal ad-Din Rumi (Iranian poet): 'Yesterday I was smart, so I wanted to change the world. Today I am wise, so I am changing myself.'

3. Big challenges are taking the world in an acceleration of consciousness growth

'Limits to Growth' is a **report by the Club of Rome** from 1972 in which the exhaustion problem is central. The report was elaborated by a team from the Massachusetts Institute of Technology (MIT) led by Dennis and Donella Meadows. It states unequivocally through scientific models that we are heading towards a global catastrophe. Reading this report in the summer of '73 gave me a sledgehammer blow on the head... But whether it changed my lifestyle much? Far too little.

So we have known for a long time that this way of dealing with the earth cannot continue. In Europe, we didn't have to worry about that. There were not so many of us killing it, because the rest of the world was hardly developed. For most of us, life only improved. Masses of people in other parts of the world supplied us with cheap raw materials and made our cheap consumer goods, which were cheaply transported to us by Eastern Europeans.

February 10, 2019, Dhaka, Bangladesh (see photos 10 and 11 on www.scienceandspirituality.be)

I have a persistent habit. Since I can find my way with a smartphone, I put a point on the map blindfolded. I drive there by public transport, and then I walk criss-cross back to encounter the unexpected. I am now in the small streets of Old Dhaka. A true maze. Here, partly on the streets, all sorts of things are manufactured. I have always greatly admired crafts and keep my eyes open: welding bicycle frames, making furniture, weaving carpets and clothes... I arrive at a small mosque and want to take a look inside, but the mosque is closed. Four young men shout rather aggressively:

- Hey, what are you going to do in our mosque?

- Well, I thought to pray.

- The mosque is closed. Every Muslim knows that now is not the time to pray. We don't believe you! (They come around me threateningly.)

- But... I am not a Muslim.

- Then what are you?

- I am a Christian by origin because I live in Europe, but for me the type of faith does not matter. There is only one God. And you can interact with that one God in any house of prayer. If you ever come to Europe, you are also welcome in our churches. We also have mosques if you prefer. (I feel the tension drop a bit but it can still go either way)

- We drink tea on that! And then we will pray together.

I follow them (although still discomforted, because the threat is not yet gone) through alleys and caverns under buildings. In those subterranean caverns, I see many children, certainly under the age of six, dyeing textiles, tanning leather... The noxious vapour from the chemicals makes my eyes water. It grabs me by the throat. I cannot resist asking:

- *Do you think it is normal for those children to work so young and in those conditions?*
- *Yes, they help their family. What would be bad about that?*

We drink tea. The images remain forever burned on my retina. For the umpteenth time, I see the excesses of our globalised neoliberal system

Then we go to the mosque together and say a fond farewell after the necessary pictures.

Seeing children working in such conditions can really depress me. A little later, I walk into the local fine arts academy. Students show me around. What boundless inspiration and creativity! Balm for the soul...

Continuing to see the whole is sometimes difficult. For the third time, I am in Dhaka. There is still grinding poverty, but much less than before. You notice that public institutions, such as a metro network, are developing. A first approach to curb suffocating air pollution. It has become a different city...

We have been rocked to sleep. And now it is hard awakening. Billions of people have been developed by that globalised economy. As a result, the world has become a better place to live for billions of people over the last thirty years. Though many people still fall by the wayside. Also in the developed part of the world such as Europe.

The problems that were already there have become huge. We suddenly notice that other parts of the earth also want oil, natural gas and other raw materials. Prices are rising because of that demand. Oh dear. We have to share. The Chinese are even buying up the forests in the Belgian Ardennes, doing the same as we do in other countries. Imagine. Development cooperation was still fun, but really sharing...?

We see people of colour in our major European cities but also in the countryside. Oh dear. It's no longer us who happily go there. They come with their products, for goodness sake... And then those heat waves and floods! Oh dear. It's no longer just us emitting greenhouse gases. It's going fast...

Raw material scarcity, refugee flows, soil pollution, disappearance of nature, biodiversity and the climate issue. We already knew it all, but we looked the other way...

Now it is clearly in front of us: if we continue like this, our species will disappear for the most part : mass extinction, but this time mankind. The 4th law of evolution! Mass extinction occurs regularly on Earth. It is in full swing!

This is the truth, but this truth leads to defeatism. Let's look at it from the perspective of evolution. The current crisis is one in the line of so many in the history of the planet. So it is not exceptional to have a crisis. But it is the first time humans have caused that crisis. And we have known for long time it will be a disaster. But there is also good news. Much better news than in previous crises. A meteorite impact was impossible for the great reptiles to fend off, causing them to become almost extinct. Now things are different: we can avert the crisis. Through consumption moderation, redistribution and circular economy, we no longer deplete the planet. And for our energy, we can easily switch to green electricity. There is one condition: we need to work together. Solar and wind energy are not constantly available everywhere. But in our deserts, there is always sunshine. And if it is night in one desert, it is day in another. There are also places with a lot of wind capacity. If it is windless in one place, it blows somewhere else. So we urgently need to link all our networks. *Together,* we do have a constant supply of energy! You can then supplement the 'world shortages' with energy storage.

Is that not good news! We can do it all! No, we should not go back to our cave. And no, we should not develop 'current' nuclear power with waste materials that will remain hazardous for another 100,000 years (!). Imagine. One hundred thousand years ago, the Neanderthals lived. And under what houses do we store this highly radioactive waste for so long, in the subsoil of our densely populated countries? And will this concrete encapsulation last that long?

This is not to say that we should not further explore better technologies without dangerous waste materials , such as nuclear fusion, but there is no new technology ready to provide electricity in the next 30 years.

So it's simple, but we have to want it. I am deeply happy with any treaty that goes in the right direction and is also global, but the real change comes from the inside. Otherwise it makes no sense. If you don't eliminate inequality first or at least simultaneously, it will never succeed. Poor people are not interested in global warming... Not even in Europe. Large income inequality leads to conflicts. Within countries, and also between countries. Conflict prevents much-needed cooperation... And no one can do it alone.

So you have to solve inequality first or at least simultaneously!

We spend 1,500 billion dollar a year on armaments on the planet. (This is $1,500,000,000,000) The European Green Deal is $100 billion a year, which is unprecedented. But European countries together spend 281 billion dollar on armaments. (This amount must be increased so that Russia doesn't overwhelm us, because they spend... $67 billion a year)

Together, the 26 richest people on earth have more wealth than the poorest half of the world's population, which is 3.8 billion people.

If we could change this...

Even without a climate crisis, you need to solve this. We know from the fourth law of evolution that crises accelerate evolution. The climate crisis will force us to use our resources not for armament but for development. The climate crisis will force us to eliminate inequality. We won't succeed otherwise. And there is no plan B. You cannot, even if you are super rich, continue to live on Mars... If the world ends, you are nothing with your money and you perish with it....

So the climate crisis is not a disaster but a blessing, like all past crises. And we have it in our own hands! A golden opportunity to take the next step in our collective consciousness.

Angela Merkel: 'Every crisis is an opportunity! '

Jalal ad-Din Rumi (Islamic poet): 'When the world pushes you to your knees you are in a perfect position to pray.'

In my own life, too, I learned that crises like the one in September 2000 (see the first chapter) are necessary to move on to the next. You prefer to run away from it, but in retrospect, a blessing. Our "personal life" runs as the 'life of humanity'...

Bible, Exodus, 11: Then Yahweh spoke to Moses: `I will send one more plague upon Pharaoh and Egypt. After that he will let you go. Finally, if he lets you go, he will even drive you away from here by force... `So speaks Yahweh: By midnight I will go around Egypt. Every firstborn in Egypt will die, from the firstborn of Pharaoh, who will succeed him on the throne, to the firstborn of the slave woman who turns the hand mill; also all the firstborn of the cattle. Then there will be loud wailing in all Egypt, as loud as there has never been and never will be again.

Egypt is here a symbol of the established order. On earth, but also within ourselves. We want everything to be preserved. Even though we know it will be a disaster. After nine plagues, Pharaoh still doesn't want change. At the tenth plague, things get so bad (his first-born dies) that Pharaoh repents. Only then do we leave our security behind and depart. Then follows a journey through the desert, full of hardships. The people sometimes want to return to the 'fleshpots' of Egypt. Finally we end up in the promised land.

Homer (Greek writer), 800 BC: Through all sorts of trials, each hiding a deep symbolism, Odysseus arrives at Ithaca, the promised land....

We should try to avoid as many 'plagues of Egypt' as possible. Time is extremely important here. Taking action as soon as possible. But you cannot direct the inside, the growth of consciousness. This consciousness has to be there, otherwise it won't work. Think of Hira, or my three pupils. And we're getting plagues upon us, they are already happening. And maybe we will go through the desert together and long for the old days again.... But we can't and won't go back to Egypt. We will arrive in the promised land. Maybe not us, but then our descendants, as in the exodus story. We arrive! This is what evolution teaches us. And you cannot change those laws. It is nature and therefore also ourselves. We are going to learn from this and receive a great gift: a new step in our collective consciousness. I am grateful to be living now and to be allowed to participate in this.

The 'inergy' rises and rises... With each higher stage of cooperation comes a higher stage of consciousness. First in biological evolution: in all organisms, billions of cells work together harmoniously, each with its own individuality. This cooperation has come about through six externally noticeable laws of evolution, but the engine is on the inside: rise in 'inergy' resulting in a more complex body with higher consciousness.

We now see the same thing in the future with humans at the level of thought: the beginning of cooperation between humans, each with their individuality. All the separate parts work together harmoniously in a 'kind of ecosystem': the earth's noosphere. That noosphere becomes a complete shell above the biosphere, atmosphere, hydrosphere, lithosphere and the hot metal core of the earth. You cannot ignore the laws of evolution, whether you want to or not. The 6 laws that formed the lithosphere and biosphere now and in the future form the noosphere. It is already happening!

Yuri Gagarin, the first human to look at the Earth from the first satellite:

'When you look at the earth from afar, you realise it is too small for conflict and just big enough for co-operation.'

'I see the earth! It is so beautiful. Space flights can't be stopped. This is not the work of one man or even a group of men. It is a historical process which mankind is carrying out in accordance with the natural laws of human development.'

May I invite you to go over your own life. Try to see a timeline. Look at your childhood. Try to recall images from that time. The kitchen, where you sat at the table with your mum, dad, brother(s) and sister(s). Then go over the rest of the years. Look at what you did well. What you got satisfaction from. Also pick out one difficult period. This could be a period after the death of someone. Or some other 'avoidable' event. Or a period of depression. Focus on that. Close your eyes and feel how this has touched you to your heart. Feel the sadness under your chest. But don't stay there. Now think about how that event changed you, shaped you. How this was absolutely necessary to be who you are today... Let this feeling flow through you. Your breathing takes over. In and out... Fully immerse yourself in the feeling that is there. Maybe it's gratitude. Maybe not...

Chapter 14:

The future of consciousness

1. People and their consciousness converge

Neurologist Dr Steven Laureys on mental wellbeing: Many non-responsive coma patients have still some form of consciousness. I used to be a rabid brain researcher, but after my divorce I fled into alcohol and pills. I had years only invested in knowledge, but with all those books and studies I couldn't do anything. Meditation put me back on track. A lot of research on Tibetan monks shows that meditation visibly changes the brain. But this research remains in the shadows because many researchers are slaves to the pharma industry. Many people are estranged from their bodies: sleep disorders, Parkinson's... Body and mind constantly influence each other. Yet many people ask for a 'quick fix': a sleeping pill, an antidepressant. They try to lull themselves to sleep or suppress their emotions, but sooner or later they resurface. We are researching how we can upgrade our brain, plug it into computers. But we pay little attention to our emotions, experiences and the intuitive. Meditation teaches you to deal with your thoughts differently. It teaches you that emotions are transitory, that you can distance yourself. We are now investigating which types of meditation are most effective for which patient, and what is the link with autohypnosis or trance? How can meditation help with cancer? And on a deeper level: what is consciousness? Where do our thoughts come from? The internal universe is infinite, just like the one outside. Meditation has made me less arrogant as a scientist. I used to think you could reduce everything to knowledge. Then I saw a rainbow and wanted to explain it. I abhor theories postulating which substances lead to which behaviours, when there is still so incredibly much we don't know at all. Can you reduce love to oxytocin or dopamine that is released? I don't think so. I love my wife and am glad I don't really know why! '

Among the nature tribes, everything is divine. This is no longer so in the modern world, due to the discovery of the immensity of the cosmos and scientific analysis. We view everything as a cog. 'Energy' is our new god. Coincidence, statistics and 'probability' explain what we do not know. Substances in our brains determine our personality, feeling and thinking. Our person disappears in this. We live on in our works, mindsets, children... This influence is extremely important but a huge waste. Because our self-consciousness is the most valuable, the essential thing in that evolution flame. We are that flame ourselves. The whole can only evolve if my 'own self-awareness' remains. The concentration of a self-conscious sphere around the earth or noosphere must collect all "self-consciousnesses", with each part remaining aware of itself (becoming more itself). The uplift of the parts reinforces the whole.

This happens just as cells in the development of the biosphere constantly differentiate further into skin cells, nerve cells, gland cells, etc. and together form a much stronger whole. Their mutual differences therefore become much greater, but they work together better and better: the organism they form becomes more and more complex. Mammals, for example, have many more types of specialised cells than cavity animals. The cells continue to exist separately: individual consciousness cannot be lost in the larger collective. But, just as in biological evolution, cells could not evolve further without other cells, we too cannot develop further without the 'others': *You cannot do without the other!*

What forces can bring people together? We should certainly look at love as the strongest force: we know partner love, friendship, parental love as a very strong bond between people, social cohesion within a nation or the whole of humanity. You can explain this by sex drive, passing on genes to your children or trading relationships with other people. But if we recognise only these 'external' ties, we never arrive at a true union of individuals. If we only see the universe as a mechanical system (which we prefer to bend to our will), we cannot feel love for it.

On **22 September 1984**, 70 years after the outbreak of World War I, French President **Mitterrand** received German

Chancellor **Kohl** with military honours in Metz. Then they flew to Verdun. Around them the fields of the great wars of the 20th century, a traumatic reminder of both men's family tragedies. In front of the Verdun charnel house was a coffin with a guard of honour of French and West German soldiers on either side. Mitterrand and Kohl stood in front of the coffin and listened to the music. First Das 'Lied vom guten Kameraden', the hymn for mourning ceremonies of the Bundeswehr, then the Deutschlandlied and the Marseillaise. After the music, Mitterrand and Kohl remained standing in the pouring rain. Suddenly Mitterrand stretched out his hand. Very hesitantly, he touched Kohl's hand. He took it. Kohl was, his own testify, 'overwhelmed' by emotions... For minutes. Like a love couple after a conflict: Verdun never again. Kohl wept at Mitterrand's funeral in 1996. Such a bond of friendship is rare in politics and has proved to be worth more than many treaties and laws.

Only the 'consciousness love ' is capable of truly uniting and completing people. The loving synthesis of individuals and peoples: only when the individual can fully unfold in the whole can the whole develop to the maximum and become stronger. (Each kind of cell has also fully developed to become a complex organism)

If you as a black, gay, transgender, woman...etc cannot reach your full potential, the consciousness of the whole of society cannot grow to its maximum opportunities. Collective 'coercion' kills the love of consciousness that would like to blossom, if it 'swallows up' the personality.

And let us not think that we have a monopoly on wisdom in Europe!

20 October 2018, Tehran, Iran
A young woman helps me find the metro station in the airport. She may have fallen, because she has a plaster on her nose. Later, I perceive many more women in the subway with such a plaster!?!! Of course, I now understand that rhinoplasties are popular here. That same evening, I look up figures for plastic surgery. Most transgender operations in the world are performed in Thailand . The second transgender country is... strict Islamic Iran! Nothing is what it seems...

23 April 2007, ferry Aswan (Egypt) - Wadi Halfa (Sudan)
(see photo 12 on www.scienceandspirituality.be)
Christine gets to sit on the mat next to two Sudanese women. They are having fun and exude great independence. Christine:
- *Why don't you wear a hijab?*
- *Oh, this is just for pictures or official things. Not really mandatory in Sudan. Is this your husband?*
- *Yes.*
- *How long have you been married to him?*
- *30 years.*

- Excuse me? It's time you change. It's more than enough with the same one!

- Are men allowed to have several wives here?

- Yes, but not with me, otherwise I would fight! Oh, all men are equal. They watch Western porn DVDs and think Westerners can give them incredible sex. Said among women: 'they are stupid creatures. If you don't like it, girl, put him at the door!

They burst out laughing and slap their thighs in delight. Christine is laughing along just a little too hard, I think.

From a Jihad of love, El Bachiri, following the death of his wife Loubna in the attack in Brussels Maalbeek metro station on 22 March 2016: *'I swear to respond to this injustice with love, as a tribute to who Loubna was and will be forever, out of esteem, admiration and love for all my human brothers and sisters, regardless of their religion, faith, origin or sexual orientation. I am Muslim but when I meet a follower of another faith who is guided by love, I feel that we profess the same religion.'*

Bible, Saint Paul's first letter to the Corinthians, 13:
'If I speak the tongues of men and of angels but have no love, I have become a resounding gong or a clanging cymbal. If I have the gift of prophesying and understand all the sacred secrets and all knowledge, and if I have the faith that can move mountains, but I have no love, then I am nothing. And if I give all my possessions to feed others, and if I give my body until dead, but I have no love, it is of no use to me at all. Love is patient and kind. Love is not envious or boastful or arrogant or rude. It does not insist on its own way; it is not irritable or resentful; it does not rejoice in wrongdoing, but rejoices in the truth. It bears all things, believes all things, hopes all things, endures all things.'

Dalai Lama: 'When we teach the brains of our youth, we must not forget to teach their hearts. '

Jalal ad-Din Rumi: 'In every religion there is love.... yet love has no religion.'

Teachers can only teach the outside. But by connecting their inner self with their students, they impart real knowledge in their discipline. You will not notice this difference in any statistics or education policy and yet everyone knows it is essential!

The noosphere can only fully develop and unite through love...

2. The future

When the noosphere is fully developed, we will no longer plunder the earth but have a circular economy. Raw materials will be reused. What we still mine is no longer the property of the people who find it under their feet, but belongs to humanity. This is also the case with water, our most important raw material. Just because more falls on your head does not mean you have more right to it than someone in the desert: we distribute it evenly through our former oil and gas pipelines. Science is no longer a 'win' activity, it is the essential development of human 'watching' and we only use it so that everyone can improve. There are no more borders. Everyone can move all over the earth, because the earth is now everyone's 'nation-state'. You can settle where you can develop, or be at the service of others. Because knowledge has also become completely free and communal. We can communicate with each other fluently via the internet, satellites, quantum computers...etc. in a common language, learned early on by everyone, and we decide, after discussion, everything globally.

We move smoothly with public or shared transport: trains, green hydrogen-powered planes... and yet there is less traffic because everyone is no longer sitting separately in their car. A street is no longer a 'road and parking space' for the 'holy car', but a meeting place. Our children play there every day and therefore have fewer mental health problems. We also no longer transport unnecessary consumption junk; we know that having more does not bring happiness.

Each community, each people is allowed to keep its individuality. Preferably even, because it is our wealth. We are not afraid of others dominating us, because no one can take away our individuality. How could they? Individuality is within. We respect 'being different' and welcome it because it brings colour and variety.

But this never happens I hear many say... Yep! It cannot be otherwise if you look at evolution and accept the evolution of the internal as the essential!

> The universe was created 13.8 billion years ago. Earth is 4.56 billion years old. If we represent development on Earth by a 24-hour day, life arises at 3.15 am. At 12am, the atmosphere becomes oxygen-rich and at 4pm the first primitive marine animals live. At 10pm, life conquers the land. The reptiles die out at 11.40 pm. The first humans are there 20 seconds before 24h. For that 'universe day', the earth took 2 days to form after the big bang.

So on those 3 'universe days', we humans live for only 20 seconds! The development of the other spheres took billions of years. We are very young. If I take the Universal Declaration of Human Rights as the 'official' beginning of the noosphere, it's about microseconds on that 72-hour scale!

We think the change is not coming because we are looking short term. And even then. The world has become a much better place to live during the last 30 years. Life expectancy, extreme poverty, education, war, discrimination... it has all improved spectacularly. In Europe, and also in many other parts of the world we no longer go to war at every turn, but we work together. (the remaining conflicts are unfortunately remnants of old thinking...)

In 1980, 85% of the world's population lived in poverty, 85% were illiterate. Now 10% are poor and 9% illiterate.
Is that sufficient? No! The numbers are still very large, and income inequality has increased sharply.

Jan Rotmans (energy transition scientist): 'Based on scientific insights, I explain in my book that the world is in a turbulent period that is irreversibly culminating in a new era where things will be extremely better. Democracy, the financial system, energy, healthcare, education, economy, industrial production and agriculture are creaking at the seams and being redesigned into versions that put people and nature at the centre. '

From 'dreamtime' (Tjukurpa), Aborigines: 'Keep your eyes on the sun and you won't see the shadows! '

We have time. We only live 20 seconds in 3 universe days... or due to global warming just not that much time anymore? Fantastic. The faster the better.

Change can happen very quickly. If we work together. Developing good vaccines against corona is an example. The genome was fully released in China. With that information, several vaccine types could be developed in a few months. Europe negotiated as a bloc with the pharma companies and promised to donate half of the vaccines. An example of cooperation! But then things turned around. Israel kept the vaccines for itself: hey guys, we're the first! The UK chased after... Beep beep, we're here too! The vaccine course was set in motion. And a little border closing game extra... Much to the delight of the pharma industry. Our leaders did not tell the truth. The truth is that you can only overcome a pandemic through vaccination if we vaccinate evenly around the world. For a virus, you cannot close any border, at most slow it down. Cooperation, solidarity. We will soon learn!

Richard Leakey, Nairobi, Kenya: 'We are developing Ngaren, a "museum of the future" that combines a physical museum in Kenya's Rift Valley with a digital platform for "state-of-the-art" science education and "storytelling".
Ngaren celebrates the beginning of all mankind. Dedicated to our shared past, Ngaren tells the story of our common ancestors, our epic journeys and our future obligation to protect the planet that is our only home. Kenya is located in the Rift Valley. Here the world will come face to face with the changes that shaped the earth and humans. And the changes needed to sustain the earth: the evolution of life is a fact! Every human being shares a common ancestor. Earth has always been a dynamic place. Stand face to face with that change. Imagine the future through your past and redefine your place in the world...'

27 May 2007, at the entrance of the closed museum in Nairobi

- *It took us three days to arrive in Nairobi in a truck belonging to the Leakey Foundation of Lake Turkana.*

- *Did you travel those three terrible days with our truck?*

- *Yes, and it was a very deep experience to undergo first-hand how remote a place on the globe can be!*

- *This is indeed very far away! Incredibly far. Wait, I'm trying to help you.*

We are taken to the head of the lab. 'Sorry sir, for scientific research only. You must have a permit from the government.'

But the African way is not exhausted yet. We talk and do the whole thing again

- *But... there's no way you can't see those fossils! This story and you two people really touched my heart! Wait, I'll call Mary'.*

With grand gestures, everything is passed on in Swahili. We nod as if we understand everything. Mary is very keen to show us around...

A world opens up. Dr. Leakey's large laboratory in operation. The fossil collection is huge. You go back in prehistory, and Mary explains to us the evolution of elephant, rhino, giraffe etc. using real fossils. We can also touch the fossils. Simply grandiose! We are incredibly grateful to be able to experience this and fall from one surprise to another.

- Scientific research is very slow here because we are just a small team. A country like Kenya has so many other priorities... Fortunately, we often get help from foreign universities, which send a team of students. Do you know that around Lake Turkana alone there are probably a hundred thousand fossils waiting to be discovered? This may further reveal the secrets of the evolution of many animal species, including humans, in the future. Turkana is such a particularly rich area because it is so hot and dry, but also because the peoples there never practised agriculture. The soil there has not been churned up, which also allowed prehistoric man's footprints to be preserved...

Bible, Revelation 21: *And I saw a new heaven and a new earth. For the former heaven and the former earth have passed away, and the sea is no more. I also saw the holy city, New Jerusalem, coming down out of heaven from God, ready as a bride adorned for her husband. Then I heard a loud voice from the throne saying, 'Look! The tent of God is with men and he will stay with them. They will be His people and God Himself will be with them. He will wipe every tear from their eyes. Death will be no more. There will be no more mourning, no crying and no more pain. The things of old are past.' He who sat on the throne said: "Look! I make everything new. He also said: "Write, for these words are trustworthy and true.' And he said to me: 'They have come true! I am the Alpha and the Omega, the beginning and the end. To everyone who is thirsty I will freely give drink from the spring of life-giving water.'*

A new heaven and a new earth. If you replace 'God' with the untold, the incomprehensible, (self-)consciousness, you notice that here too the writer (apostle John) knows that only through a rise of the inner energy, the inside, consciousness, the change to a 'new earth' can happen.

Mamphela Ramphele, co-chairwoman at the current Club of Rome: 'When I saw the 1972 report, I read little understanding of Africa. The focus on Europe and the US showed the narrow spirit of that time. The described environmental and food problems in Africa or Latin America were not caused by Africans but by the greed after colonial conquests. As the birthing room of humanity, however, Africa had already developed highly sustainable forms of life before that. It is no coincidence that in the philosophy of Ubuntu, originated in Africa, the essence is that we are all connected and dependent on each other. So the Africans had long known that there were limits to growth or that there are enough natural resources for everyone if you use them sustainably. We knew for generations that over-cultivation, over-harvesting, and unlimited mining for the sake of profit would get us into trouble. Knowledge and science alone are insufficient for radical changes. You can only achieve transition if you can change people's mindsets. A 'human revolution', making us aware that our sustainability and well-being is connected to the whole web of life. This was our way of life before it was disrupted by slavery and corrupt leadership.'

Chapter 15

String theory or M-theory: more dimensions. In search of the supra-personal

Thomas Aquinas: *' If the highest aim of a captain were to preserve his ship, he would keep it in the port forever.'*

1. Near-death experiences

So, to recap. When closely examined within the atom, electrons and protons have no exact location (=non local): they are represented by a wave, and 'flow' around everywhere, just like a radio wave. A radio wave can be in many places at once. (When you switch on a radio set, you can receive that wave in many places and separate the sound wave.) Only when observed does the particle make a 'choice'. And only our averages obey the physical laws. So particles are 'non-local'. But particles apparently also 'know' something. They are directed. This research is in its infancy, but we already know for sure that in the cell, atoms 'target' each other to react. We also already know that mutations that drive our evolution are not blind coincidence. Particles 'know' something, have information. We don't recognise this as consciousness. But we have seen that the 'working together' of atoms can make substances that are more complicated. We don't recognise this as consciousness either. When that cooperation goes on continuously, we suddenly do see it: life. And we recognise that very well. We know that a coronavirus is alive! We don't recognise consciousness there either. As life forms become more complicated, we have to recognise: in higher animal species, there is consciousness. Those animals 'know' something. In humans, you can no longer ignore it: a human being doesn't just 'know' something. He 'knows that he knows': self-awareness. This is not a detail. It makes a human being what he is. It is essential.

Most scientists believe that you can locate a person's self-awareness in the brain. But there is no evidence for this.

From Endless Consciousness (Pim Van Lommel): ′When the bleeding did not stop, Bill knew he was going to die. "I passed away, but I was completely at ease. There was a golden light, brighter than the sun, but it didn't hurt my eyes. I wanted nothing more than to enter into that light, but something or someone - it seemed to be my father, who died when I was a child - said to me, 'It's not your time yet. You have to go back to finish what you have to do in your life'. In the next moment, I was thrown back into my body. It felt like a wet sock and the pain was terrible. ′

An example of a description of a near-death experience.

In 2001, cardiologist Pim van Lommel published a study of 344 Dutch patients about their near-death experience. In people who are clinically dead, no brain activity is measured at all. You only see a straight line on the screen and not a wave or spike. This is incompatible with near-death experiences which, on the contrary, testify to an extremely broad awareness. Some people can also tell exactly what was said, what happened in the surgery room, during their 'dead' period. No scientific explanation can adequately explain this.

Anja Opdebeeck : 'I will be the last to deny that a near-death experience can be partly explained psychological, neurophysiological or pharmacological. Those are all facets. But put them all side by side, and you will come to the conclusion that there is still a facet missing.'

Carl Jung suffered a heart attack in 1944, followed by a near-death experience: (from Memories, Dreams, Thoughts). 'It seemed as if I were high, above in the world's space; far below me I saw the globe, dipped in a glorious, blue light. I saw the deep blue sea and the continents. Far below my feet laid Ceylon and in front of me was the subcontinent of India. My field of vision did not encompass the entire earth, but its spherical shape was clearly recognisable; its contours danced silvery through the wondrous, blue light. In some places, the earth appeared colourful or mottled dark green, like oxidised silver. To the left, in the distance was a vast plain, the reddish-yellow desert of Arabia. It seemed if the silver of the Earth had turned a red-gold color there. Then came the Red Sea, and very far in the distance, about 'top left', I could just make out a small piece of the Mediterranean Sea. Mainly on that spot I had fixed my gaze; everything else appeared only unclear. Although I also saw the snowy mountains of the Himalayas, it was misty or cloudy there. To the right I did not look. I knew I was about to leave the earth. Later, I found out how high you have to be in space to have such a distant view: about 1500 km! The sight of Earth from this height was the most glorious thing I had ever seen. After contemplating all this for some time, I turned around. I had, so to speak, been standing with my back to the Indian Ocean and my face to the north.

I felt as if everything I had experienced until then was taken away from me. All my opinions, my wishes and thoughts, the whole phantasmagoria of earthly existence fell away from me, or was stolen from me. An extremely painful process, but something also remained, because it was as if everything I had ever experienced or done, everything that had happened around me, was now with me. I could also say: it was with me and that was 'me'. I consisted of it, so to speak. I existed out of my past and definitely felt like, 'that's me' now? I am this bundle of what has been accomplished and what has been...' This experience gave me the feeling of extreme poverty, but at the same time of great satisfaction....

It seemed like my life had been cut out with scissors of a long chain, and many questions were left unanswered. Why did it happen this way? Why did I bring these starting points with me? What have I done with them? What will come out of this? All these questions, I was sure, would be answered soon once I entered the stone temple. There I would see why everything had been so and not otherwise. There I would join the people who knew the answers to my questions about the before and the after... It was protested that I was about to go. I was not allowed to leave earth and had to return. The moment I heard that, the vision, my near-death experience ended. I was deeply disappointed, because now everything seemed to be vainly. The painful process of 'defoliation' had been in vain and I was not allowed to enter the temple, not to the people who belonged to me. In reality, more than 3 weeks passed before I could decide to live again. I did not eat because all food repulsed me. The view of the city and mountains from my sickbed seemed like a painted curtain with holes, or a newspaper full of holes and with pictures that meant nothing to me. Disappointed, I thought, now I have to go back into the 'box system'! It seemed to me as if behind the horizon of the cosmos a three-dimensional world had been artificially constructed, where each person sat alone in a box for himself. And now I would have to imagine again that that was worth something! Life and the whole world seemed like a prison to me, and I was boundlessly annoyed that I should find that quite normal again. I had just been so happy that finally everything had fallen away from me, and now it was again as if I was, like all other people, hanged on by wires inside a box. Standing in space, I was weightless and nothing had pulled at me. And that was supposed to be over by now! Silently I blamed my doctor for bringing me back to life.... '

I myself have met death twice in the sea:

Oostende, July 1961

As a 6-year-old child, I float slowly into the sea with my sister and two cousins. We can't get back. I see the beach getting smaller and smaller, helplessly floating around in panicked fear...

Menton, southern France, 12 April 2002

I like to swim in high surf. Too high, this time... I can't make it back to shore... Every minute, meter-high waves crash over me, completely engulf me and spin me around. I am their plaything and I constantly swallow water. While I'm still gasping for breath and almost coughing out my lungs from the cold, salty water, after a metre-high wall, the next wave is already looming with its destructive brutal fist... The sea water is still very cold in April, I feel my body getting hypothermic and life draining away. I see Christine standing on the beach in the rain, she does not realise I'm in trouble. It's for the last time I see her because it's the end, my muscles can't fight anymore. Everything becomes hazy around me, dying is not difficult: you slide further into the water in stupor. One or maybe two more waves... A huge calm comes over me. But the next waves don't swallow me whole... The wind has just dropped a little, allowing me to use my final strength to throw myself on the beach. I grab onto the sand and boulders, but can't get up. I see Christine running towards me. I will live on...

I certainly don't consider that event a near-death experience, but since that day, I know that there is a great peace that comes before you die, even in such turbulent circumstances. So I cannot feel any fear at all for my greatest journey.

Testimonies about near-death experiences are so massive that you can no longer ignore them... The testimonies also tell facts that cannot originate as hallucinations. How can Carl Jung describe the earth so perfectly, when his description was confirmed by the first satellites only 20 years later? Moreover, at the moment of that 'dilated experience of consciousness', an EEG of the brain shows a flat line: no brain activity at all....

Although something is clearly wrong here, resistance in strictly scientific circles is very reluctant to accept this. Of course, this has always been the case with any new theory that shakes the existing sciences. Think of evolutionary theory, continental drift or quantum mechanics.

Let's think about that further...

Particles are non-local within the atom. We know that. Recently, we also know that living systems use the bizarre quantum mechanical phenomena. For example, non-locality. Why couldn't consciousness also be non-local, if particles certainly are? We have never been able to prove consciousness scientifically in the brain...

After all, we cannot (yet) measure consciousness. Why can't science accept that there are aspects to a near-death experience that are unexplainable? Why should that consciousness be lost when you die, when even any form of 'measurable energy' in a system is never lost according to the first law of thermodynamics? Energy is simply transformed into other forms in a closed system.

> **Albert Einstein:** 'Time exists only to prevent everything from happening at once.'

We know that time is an 'illusion', and tied to matter. Why couldn't our consciousness be timeless?

Why could our consciousness not be non-local and timeless if that has already been proven for the universe and the inside of matter?

In this art piece, I try to express that even when we have worries, our consciousness is always accompanying us, standing 'behind' us.

2. String theories and M-theory

The mathematical models of quantum mechanics and the theory of relativity contradict each other. The great challenge now is to develop a theory in physics, to unite the theory of the very small (quantum mechanics) and the very large (the theory of relativity) into one. There can be only one truth. This has led to the development of several 'string theories'. (Particles are no longer represented by points, but by tiny, vibrating strings.) These are then united in the M-theory (particles are represented by little membranes). The relativity theory assumed four variable dimensions: length, width, depth and time. Here our imagination already falls short. The various string theories assume 9 or 10 dimensions....

We might be able to express this into a mathematical model, but really understand it? Able to imagine it?

So how could something as complicated as an eye have come into existence by chance? Or humans? The universe? The fully balanced biosphere?

Isn't it totally illogical to attribute this to 'coincidence' as classical science says? Isn't it much more scientific and logical to look for a deeper meaning, a purpose behind it all?

Albert Einstein: 'If this universe, in its millionfold order and precision, were the result of blind chance, it would be as credible as if a printing house exploded and all the printing letters happened to end up back on the floor in the perfect and flawless form of the dictionary.'

Now let's explore further possibilities. Why can't one or more of those at least 9 dimensions, which we can calculate in string theories, have to do with consciousness?

Or life energy, not measurable, but so recognisable to us...

Or love energy: also for us not scientifically measurable, not to be classified among the 'known energies', but the strength of that energy (is energy a good word for that?)... yes, you don't need a drawing for that.

So does that mean that this reality is not there because we cannot demonstrate it?

That the 6 remaining dimensions in string theories are not there because we cannot prove them now?

It is important to see here that exact science is not that exact at all. We work with averages and models. We need those models to work with. But our model ís not reality. Some aspects of reality behave like our model. Reality is different. An electron ís not a wave or particle, but 'behaves' like a wave or particle. A wave, a particle, is our brain image, our imagination.

We imagine an electron as a particle, string or wave, but the real reality...? And the models we use in science describe only 4% of the matter in the universe (see chapter 3.1 p 45), the rest is   invisible? What then is that other 96%? Those other dimensions?

> **Plato**: 'In life, we are like in a cave, taking the shadows on the wall from outside as reality. The real reality takes place outside the cave.'

We must continue to know that reality is outside the cave. We have only the 'reflection' , a glimpse of reality, to picture it. This is very difficult and reality will always remain incomplete and incomprehensible....

In any religion or philosophy of life, as well as in science, reality is not exactly as described. Images, metaphors are used, representing a reality that cannot be understood. In the sciences, these images are increasingly becoming mathematical models. They are the 'images of science'. Science thus has all the characteristics of a religion. Images are very valuable. We can't do without them. They are 'real' for us. Just like the Via Dolorosa or the Camino de Santiago or Bohr's atomic model. But they are not the full reality. They are adapted to our mind, our humanity. So contradictory images can both be true! (Think of the particle and wave model for light) Let us embrace all myths, sagas, legends, holy books, scientific models... It is our unimaginable wealth...!

Unless images or theories stand in the way of the evolution of loving humanity... In that case, classify them as an earlier side branch of the many dead-end branches of the evolution of thought.

November 2016 Dompu, Indonesia: A chance encounter on the ferry led me to an Islamic project for problem youth on Sumbawa island. I have been living with them for just under a week now. They get lessons, but also do something in return for the community: cleaning up all the plastic rubbish has washed up on Sumbawa's beaches. They sort it and then sell it as raw material for the organisation's operation. We also pray four times a day in the small mosque. When an Islamic text is read aloud, I can almost always retrieve a similar Christian meditation text from my smartphone. We take turns reading aloud and come away impressed by the similarity of each other's wisdom... It is for me one of the most profound experiences ever...

3. Contact with the **common**

Consciousness and the ability to remember things are older than humans. Before intelligent life existed on Earth, there was already a virus that had this ability. Through infection from this virus, our arc gene is thought to have arisen. This gene is responsible for our long-term memory. So did viruses have a viral collective memory many millions of years ago? Our arc gene is crucial for the ability to learn.

Albert Einstein: 'If I were not a physicist, I would probably be a musician. I often think in music. I live my daydreams in music. I see my life in terms of music. '

Einstein did not experience music 'alongside' it, but it was an integral part of his life and work: 'The greatest scientists are artists as well'. Everything is related and interacts with each other. The secret of a genius can be attributed to finding 'coherence' in seemingly 'incoherent things'. That we sometimes have a different perception of this may very well be due to upbringing. Even in our early childhood, we are trained to 'specialise' and during our schooling and education we are learn mathematics without music, science without images, feelings and intuitions. Knowledge without imagination.

Albert Einstein: 'The theory of relativity came to me through intuition, and music is the driving force behind this intuition . My parents made me study violin from the age of six. My new discovery is the result of musical perception. Examining myself and my way of thinking, I come close to the conclusion that the gift of imagination has meant more to me than any talent for absorbing absolute knowledge.'

I close the Aboriginal book 'Dreamtime'. How beautiful. The way of dealing with nature. That extremely difficult nature to survive in. Did that complicated way of life come about only by chance and natural selection? It certainly played a part. But it cannot be the full explanation.

Somehow, information has been captured. Aborigines explain this phenomenon in having contact with their ancestors through 'dreamings'. By those 'dreamings', the system for survival in those extremely difficult conditions was communicated. Those people do not need scientific explanations.

What is inspiration? Where does it come from? I think again of the man from Peshawar. (Chapter 1)

The meaning of the word 'inspiration' comes from the Latin word 'inspirare', which literally means 'to inhale' or 'to breathe in'. It means to blow in the soul or spirit. The dictionary gives also the word 'animation' (animo means soul). It also recognises the word 'spiritus'. Spiritus is translated as spirit or soul.

Inspiration is needed for the images of the many myths, religions, which are often very similar. Science has different images for the same...

There is 'something in common' we can draw from. That muse whispering in your ear....

The theory of evolution or the theory of relativity was brewing in many places

Jung describes 'the collective unconscious'. And, of course, there is also a collective consciousness: As a people, as humanity, we are aware of a common history, common values. There is also the nascent noosphere...

> **Carl Jung**: 'The unconscious is not only evil in nature, it is also the source of the highest good. Not only dark but also light, not only half-human and demonic but also superhuman, spiritual and in the classic sense of the word: divine. '

Through nature, meditation, prayer, art or music, we can get in touch with what we have in 'common'. So you have to be able to create quiet. This is difficult for everyone, and not just in our digital age.

Guido Gezelle (1830 - 1899) puts it this way: (gij badt op eenen berg alleen)

> You prayed upon a mount alone,
> and, Jesus, I discover none
> where I may climb so highly
> and you alone be finding :
> the world will ever after me
> where I may flee
> or be
> or where my eyes may see ;

Nor does our personal self-consciousness disappear. There is no culture other than the Western that does not know that self-consciousness continues to exist, although we in Europe know better than anyone else that energy and mass can be converted to each other, that time is a product of matter and at least parts of that matter are not bound to one 'place'.

Jalal ad-Din Rumi: 'Do not grieve. Everything you lose comes back to you in another form.'

24 February 2019 Varanasi India

Because I can't resist swimming in the Ganges River in the morning and evening, I got to know Dhanesh:

- You became a friend in those few days because through our conversations we could see a glimpse of each other's souls. It is a gift from the holy Ganges River. This evening I will not come to bathe at this place because my uncle is being cremated. May I invite you to also be present and

accompany him with your spirituality and that of your people?

- Okay, I'll be there...

I stay in the background as much as possible in the evening because I don't want to disturb the family event. Yet you get totally absorbed in it. I am deeply impressed by how death is handled here. Nothing is hidden. Yes, there is grief, but also joy and gratitude for the past life. The eldest son ignites the pyre. We see the remains disappear into the air and the Ganges. The body is given back to the earth. For Dhanesh, it is not even a question of whether there is anything after death

Michael Palin: 'One of the difficult things of travelling is to say goodbye.'

Is it important what images you need to fathom reality? Whether you call this God or not? Let's hold each other's hands. All people of good will. Deep believers. In the human project. Let us make a human chain across the planet. Over and over, and feel the love that can save us. Only with rules and laws it will never succeed. But with the enormous power (or should I say energy or 'inergy'?) of love, it can be done. We all have it in us. We are lovers, parents, teachers, etc. None of that can exist without it. Love is much stronger than hate: a jihad of love... Keep holding hands and unite our little loves into one big entity.

Paris September 2, 2022

Christine and I are in Paris with our 10 grandchildren. We try to get them excited about the beautiful sculpture in the city. Quite difficult. That's why we only focus on 3 sculptures around a story: Cain and Abel.

We encounter a first one in the 'Petit Palais': 'The First Burial'(E Barrias): Adam and Eve mourn their murdered son Abel. The lifeless body lies in their arms. The image grabs you by the throat because it expresses such a primal emotion: losing a child as a parent is about the greatest possible suffering.

- Did that really happen?

- No way, replies everyone.

- So why is it in the Bible?

- Oh, grandpa, this we don't know...

- Well, Cain and Abel are actually two parts within yourself. Abel means 'breath, vapour'. He represents the spirit within us, the inspiration and intuitive guidance that comes to us when we can open up to it. So it is the spiritual part within us. The Cain in us is impatient, trying to make things happen even when we know it is not good for the whole. It kills our spiritual guidance and chooses personal desires.

Cain is not punished by God in the story but afterwards founded the city of Nod. (Nod means aimlessness) Only pursuing personal desires ends in aimlessness.

An hour later, we arrive in the 'Jardin des Tuileries' at another beautiful sculpture: 'Cain has just killed his brother Abel.'(H. Vidal) We see the suffering Cain. The Cain in us is cause of much suffering in ourselves. This sculpture is also magnificent and evokes a lot of emotion. Christine tells the children:

'If you get a nice, spontaneous idea and reject it, Cain kills Abel. If you ignore the desire to forgive, Cain kills Abel. Every time a desire to overcome an unwanted habit is refused, Cain kills Abel. Cain kills many Abels in us. But the beauty of it is that there will always be a new opportunity, a new child will be born: Adam and Eve then bore Seth (Seth means substitute). The spiritual will always reassert itself, both in our lives and on the earth...

The children's attention is drawn to a giant painting of the 'Good Samaritan' (Petit Palais, A Morot). They know the story, and understand that those three people also had a choice between Cain and Abel, and that the Samaritan, the least esteemed of the three, was the only one who chose Abel.

We will have to transcend our own little Cain to solve the big world problems.

The third sculpture group (P Landowski), a little further in the 'Tuileries' depicts the 'sons of Cain': Jabel the shepherd, Jubal the poet and Tubalcain the blacksmith.

'The artist was inspired by 3 young Tunisians, brotherly united and represents all of humanity, brotherly united.'

Cain is 'evil' to our human judgment. And that's how it should be. But that's a human judgment. We view the history of humanity and the cosmos as the underside of a knotted Iranian carpet: only disorderly knots. Only aimlessness (Nod). We only see the powerful mystical pattern when turning around. 'Evil, suffering' ultimately brings further evolution. (Seth) Think about personal crises, mass extinctions. Or neoliberalism, globalization… All not desirable and not fun, but everything works out in the end. (It is something completely different if you elevate this to 'intention', as has happened with neoliberalism, for example)

> The 'Obelisque' on 'Place de la Concorde' is not only the oldest 'stone' in the city of Paris, just about everywhere in the area you can find Egyptian symbols.

The discovery of the 'Rosetta Stone' in Napoleon's time suddenly made it possible to decipher many ancient Egyptian texts. In the book 'The Pagan Christ', Tom Harpur shows that almost all Bible stories, often in great detail, already existed in ancient Egypt. Long before the arrival of Jesus, Egyptians and other ancient peoples believed in the coming of a messiah, a madonna and her child and a virgin birth. All figures are mythical and often even older. Abraham is Brahman, the God of Hinduism, the oldest world religion.

In Hiduism, Brahman, Vishnu and Shiva form the 'Christian Trinity'

The resurrection of Lazarus is depicted in hieroglyphics down to the smallest details (including the names of his sisters Mary and Martha).

Let us consider this further. Are historical facts really that 'real'? We all know that historical writing is highly coloured, depending on the source. Myths, on the other hand, reflect a universal, deeper reality. Thanks to quantum mechanics, we also know by now that the 'images of science' are not 'reality' either, but describe a deeper 'real' that cannot be put into literal words.

> Tom Harpur in 'The Pagan Christ': 'Throw away the myth and you lose everything. '

If the images of science trigger something in you, embrace them as a scientist. Can the goodness of man touch you, embrace that humanity as a humanist. Can the images of Christianity, Buddhism, Islam... inspire your Abel , then embrace them. But never take your images as literally historical and never think that your wisdom is also that of someone else. Let's look and listen to each other. In every vision of life, you will notice that there is more than we can understand. And the whole is more than the sum of all that all. We can learn so much from each other.

And we need images, myths. They are so much richer than historical facts. They bridge the gap to a deeper reality that cannot be put into words. Even the biblical images of Christianity or the models of science are debunked by taking them literally, and then seeing that they are historically inaccurate.

We have forgotten what humanity has always known: the myth is our reality, the way home.

The Polynesian culture does not distinguish between myths and historical facts.

Pope Francis: 'You don't have to believe in God to be a good person. In a sense, the traditional notion of God is outdated. One can be spiritual but not religious. There is no need to go to church and donate money. For many, nature is a church. Some of the best people in history did not believe in God, while some of the worst acts were in His name.'

In our earthly reality, evolution is a fact. But... evolution means change over time! And... we know that time is an illusion... Earthly reality behaves according to those laws, but those laws are not the full reality!

Carl Jung: 'He who looks outside is dreaming, he who looks inside is waking up.'

I have become convinced, like Carl Jung, that the cultures which I have been in close contact with in Asia and Africa have more access to this common ground than European people. Something is lost in industrial development. We know it from the sixth law of evolution: if you focus too much on the outside and specialise too much, you cannot evolve further. The real evolution is on the inside. So I often see a much greater life force, life energy, in other peoples...

We also experiencing it in our super-specialised global economy. If one cog gets stuck in a production system...

A British anthropologist studied the Maori in 1905: He noticed that everyone built their own boat. Some could do it much better than others. So he asked the chief: *'Wouldn't it be interesting if the people who are good at building boats did this for everyone? Others can then take care of fishing. That fishing will be better, with better boats'.*

The chief reflected, smiled and spoke: *'How boring life would be, if you did the same thing all the time. You would only feed one piece of your soul...'*

11 January 2007, Jakarta, Indonesia
(see photo 13 on www.scienceandspirituality.be)
The old harbour district. There is no metro here, so we take the 'economy-train'. Which is to say: almost free, overcrowded, dirty, but real. Don't miss a ride like this. People want to sell you everything, beggars pass by, children crawl between your feet, the noise is unbearable. Doors are never closed. Too hot , and such an incredible ant nest. Perhaps someone regularly falls out of that train? Central Jakarta is... living with all of Belgium in Bruges together. I cannot possibly describe the chaos here. The many canals to the sea are open sewers. People live in hovels at the edge of this stinking water. Dirt floats everywhere: plastic bags, cardboard...The crowds, the

traffic. How can you live here? And yet. Under the bridge, just next to the dirt, a young man is washing himself. You can just see it through a crack in the road surface. He will come out of this shack immaculate clean. People on the street have a calm, friendly look... How do they do it? Where do a lot of them get this resilience?

A group of schoolchildren is very happy to interview us. An assignment for the English teacher. A photo is also part of it.

The old fishers quarter is even more chaotic. The water stinks like hell. Dirt is everywhere. People gawk at us, looking at the pale colour of our eyes. Children run after us. Not completely at our ease. But the same again: that incredible life force in every glance. Fire in the eyes. Kindness: 'mister, mister...' We walk back to the train station and encounter again a group of students with an almost desperate look: 'we haven't met anyone to interview in English yet...' We patiently answer all the questions again with lots of fun inside. Photo too. What fun they will have when both groups see in their English lesson that they asked the same people, the same questions! We ride back on the overcrowded, heated train. Four children make music in our compartment (a better word is cargo box with handles on the ceiling) and sing the soul out of their body. It is delightful and rises straight to the heart. These 'chicos' are made for guitar and drums. The wagon is more beautiful to me now than the concert hall in Bruges...

People have an unbelievable warmth in them that engulfs your soul. You know you miss this a bit (a lot) in Europe....

Bangkok, January 12, 2004, Thailand

We are on the commuter train, riding out of Bangkok. I'm still a bit sleepy. Christine:

- Do you feel that depressed atmosphere? It is exactly like with us, here. Everyone sits staring blankly ahead.

- I notice it too. And it is indeed true. Something is lost when you look around in a more developed society.

- Yes, the connection is no longer there! You see, as with us, aimlessness on many faces. Although people have it materially a lot better here.

All great scientists were in touch with this 'common', this inside, this inspiration, this creativity... We cannot do without this inside... If we haven't seen that from the story of evolution....

Why couldn't all these separate 'self-consciousnesses' become more and more unified, as happened in the lithosphere and biosphere? Why should the laws of evolution suddenly change now? If you accept the laws of evolution, it can't be otherwise than that one day all self-consciousness will have flown completely together into one big whole: the noosphere. And why could the driving force for that evolution, for that noosphere not be the universal love as all religions and also humanism claim? Why could that universal love and that new dimension of the noosphere not be found in one or more of those dimensions of the string theories or M-theory?

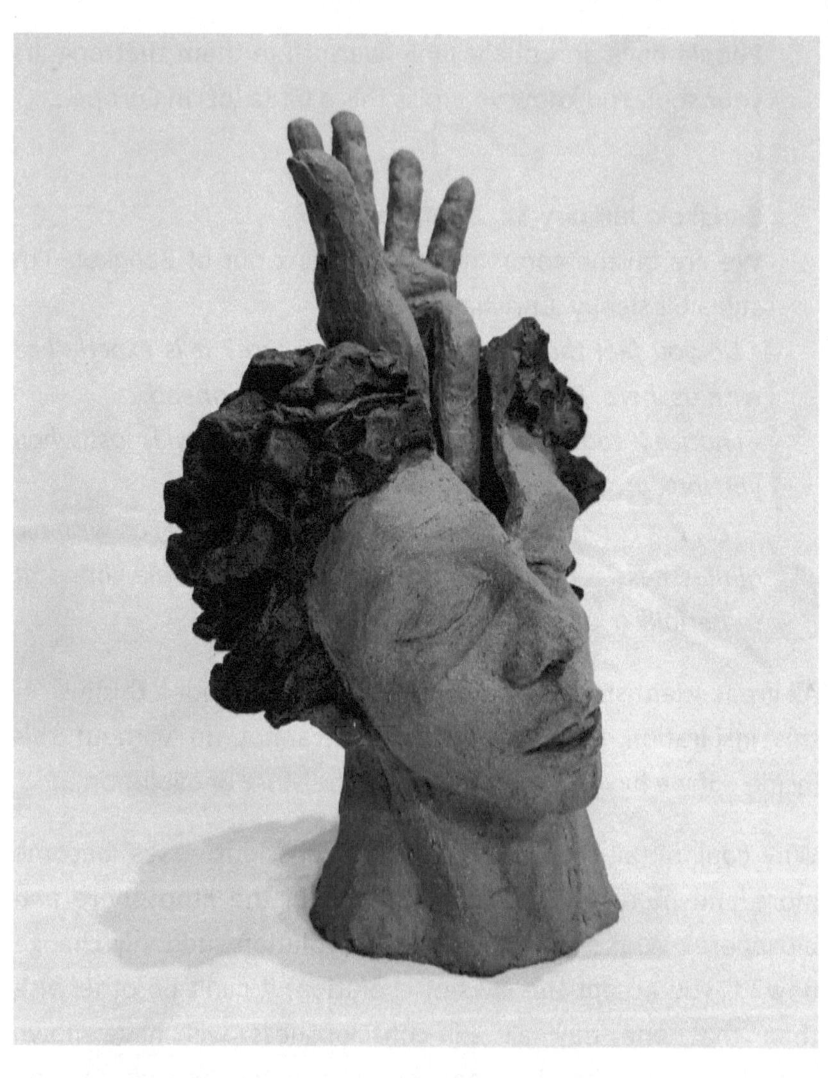

in this sculpture, I try to express human creativity. The connection to the collective consciousness.

4. Contact with other life in the universe

There may be other concentrations of consciousness in the universe. Even if we can fly at speeds approaching the speed of light, even then it is inconceivable that we will ever come into physical contact with those other self-conscious beings. But if our 'consciousnesses' form a powerful noosphere and our personal consciousness is yet much higher than now, perhaps other possibilities will arise. Perhaps teleportation might be possible then? If two 'paired particles' can do it?

A bright future awaits us and the universe!

> **From 'Dreamtime', Aborigines**: 'We are all visitors to this place and time. We are just passing by. We are in transit. Our purpose here is to observe, to learn, to grow, to love,... And then, we return home...!'

May I invite you to close your eyes and reflect on our earthly visit. We get a chance on our journey here to contribute to this beautiful place. Life passes quickly. Soon you will be dead and leave everything behind. Maybe as early as tomorrow, or a little later. Looking back on my past life, could I observe, learn, grow and love? Do I want to observe, learn, grow and love even more intensely from today before I go back home?

Try to connect with the self-awareness of your parents and grandparents, with that of all people, living on earth or in another dimension, the collective consciousness. Ask for inspiration...

Afterword: 22 February 2022, Hontanas, Camino Francés, Spain

Things have come full circle. I am back on the Camino. It is hot, the meseta (high plateau of gently rolling hills) after Burgos shimmers in the afternoon sun. Hontanas seems like a ghost village again, like in 1993. Because of the pandemic. A woman gives me a drink, someone else a piece of home-baked apple cake: *'Buen Camino...'Muchas gracias...'* , grateful for what I was allowed to write this winter. This book, certainly not 'my words'... I have been given them. At unexpected moments. Often in the wee hours. Or on the bike, quickly jotting down something. And on the Camino, of course. Inspiration..., undirectable. You are helped, you are guided... Sometimes the connection succeeds, very often not. So many times I completely stopped writing. Out of impatience. Because my faith and trust are not that great.

Ok, we often fall back into the same thing, but we learn, we evolve. The next 'turn of the circle' is not the same, but reaches a higher level of consciousness: a spiral. So, the 'circle' is not round but 'a spiral'. Evolution is de-folding, de-velopment, where instead of 'de-' you can also read 'out-'. Something that was not visible before, emerges 'from' the 'folds'. It unwinds. Like from a small seed a big plant emerges. What becomes that plant is present in that seed. From the seed of the big bang, the universe unfolds, with on earth people who 'know that they know': the searching spearhead in that evolution. Evolution is a process. Not an result. Playful and flexible from the very beginning. Rigid structures (like a crystal) or over-specialisation are a dead end.

We see all around us how the universe and also the world is evolving. Heraclitus of Ephesus (5th century BC): *'Everything that exists is in motion and nothing is permanent'*. We notice how in nature everything changes. We notice how we ourselves change. Music, painting, literature, technology, science, so our whole culture changes incessantly. This happens, as in our own life, in a process of disappearing and appearing, of death and birth, passing on the essence: the internal, consciousness.

Until humanity, evolution was locked in matter (instinct, inner drive). With the appearance of self-awareness, this determinedness passed into responsibility. The time of self-evolution has arrived. We are taking evolution into our own hands and are moving towards one noosphere: greater unity in diversity each time. Traffic and telecommunication form one nervous system. In scientific research, there is already global cooperation. Scientists are feverishly working to make the 'inner' of matter visible: consciousness and matter are one. If this is developed further, and it will be in the future, the division between science, humanism and religion will fade. Because, essentially, they are the same. Only different images are used.

So this book is a strong plea for connection. Between people, views and cultures. Our own evolution teaches us that this is the future. Quantum mechanical thinking teaches us that opposing views can both be true, necessary. Loving respect for other opinions is more important than being right: we need each other to survive on earth. Working together is our success. No longer per country now, but across the entire planet. Let us measure all political decisions, all news reports, everything we undertake, against this one idea: does it bring humanity closer together? Does it connect us lovingly? Super. If so, we follow our inner evolutionary path to higher self-awareness. And then we can handle anything.

> **Michael Palin**: *'Contrary to what some politicians and religious leaders would like us to believe, the world won't be made safer by creating barriers between people. The complexity and diversity of the world is the hope for the future.'*

And we know that this self-awareness is not bound to matter, and is therefore timeless... You and I have always existed and we will always continue to exist: timeless cores of consciousness in evolution.

Hold each other's hands for a beautiful earth for our children. I am thinking of my own children and their partners: Koenraad, Ine, Nele, Linus, Goedele, Didier, Roeland and Elke.
And for our grandchildren: Jarne, Hilke, Lobke, Nore, Liene, Ilan, Ana, Tiemen, Robbe and Seppe.

An earth where everyone can fully develop their person according to their inner consciousness. Just as all living things form a wonderfully harmonious biosphere, our self-awareness grows feverishly towards an at least equally wonderfully harmonious noosphere. It is irreversible, though we often suffer growing pains... It happens sooner than you think!

Take from the thoughts of this book what is for you, and build your own home with it. Good luck! *'Buen Camino...!'*

Johan Germonpré

Word of thanks

July 1986, Barret-Le-Bas, Provence, southern France
We have been camping by a small river with the children for a few days now. We already stayed in several places in the high mountains on that trip, because staying in one place is not for me. I am too restless for that. I am now 31 years old and could be satisfied with my life. A beautiful family with four children. Successful as a teacher. But still the inner turmoil remains. I am searching. For years I have been looking for answers that I don't find. I am Catholic and educated as a scientist but cannot reconcile the two. Science provides answers that are at odds with what I learned from my parents, and from the many religion lessons at school. The religion lessons. Apart from the beautiful Bible stories, I can't recount much about it anymore. One something. A name. 'Teiaar De Jardin'. That name has been mentioned a few times in religion class. In the fourth year of my secondary school. Why the name stuck with me, I don't know, but it has to do with faith and science. In the catalogue trays of the Bruges library, I have been searching the sheets for quite some time, for 'D', 'J' and 'T'. But I can't find anything. I also made enquiries in several bookstores. Nobody knows a writer 'Teiaar De Jardin'. Until last week. 'But... that's not Teiaar De Jardin! That might be 'Pierre Teilhard de Chardin!' His main work is 'The phenomenon of man'. 'Shall I order it for you?' It is published in Dutch in the scientific 'Aula series'.

Three days later, I have the work with me on our camping trip. A godsend. It makes the holiday with the kids the best trip ever because I finally find answers to questions I have bothered me for so long. I struggle through this book on this camping holiday. A masterpiece that has never left me. It has become a part of my thinking and being. Also in my biology lessons. I completely re-read it to write this book. Large parts of this book are a modern written-out version of 'The phenomenon of man', supplemented with new scientific insights. While writing this book, I am certain that he stood beside me and looked over my shoulder, inspired me, driving me on when I was at the end of my rope. I am unimaginably grateful to that man, who died in exile on Easter 1955, but whom I am sure is still there.

And further...

This book would never have come about, without the help, advice and patience of a lot of people:

Pieter Vandierendonck convinced me to write.

Without the continued support of Christine Goethals, my dear wife, this book would never have been realised. She continued to inspire and stimulate me and came up with the title of the book.

Didier Lecluyse, Goedele Germonpré, Katrien Vandendriessche, Koen Vandendriessche and Nele Germonpré, read the work carefully. They constantly gave me advice, encouraged me to continue writing when I was at a loss and pointed out content deficiencies and formal errors.

Nele Germonpré designed the cover.

Didier Lecluyse and Joost Dancet conceived the Dutch and English website.

With the help, encouragement and layout of Koen Vandendriessche, the Dutch project was finally completed.

Boudewijn Verhelst, former Belgian diplomate, made a first correction of the English translation.

Special thanks to Paul Bentley, Editor of the British Teilhard Network website in the UK. His positive response to the book and his offer to double check the translation encouraged me to continue to believe in the English translation.

To all these people: thank you very much!

Glossary

Camino Francès: it's the most famous pilgrimage route in Europe: from the town of St. Jean Pied de Port in France to Santiago de Compostela in Spain. (790km or 490miles) This route is walked by hundreds of thousands of pilgrims every year from over the whole world.

Chromosome: consists of one long DNA molecule, in the shape of double helix (a kind of spiral staircase) Each DNA molecule consists of 4 types of nucleotides.

Coherence: cohesion, the connection of two particles (these can be atoms, protons, electrons, photons....).

Collective unconscious (Jung): Our personal consciousness consists of two parts. A conscious and an unconscious part and is there thanks to one's own experiences. The collective unconscious is inherited. The human mind is predestined by brain and body through evolution. The brain is the primary organ of the mind. Because of this, the collective unconscious depends on the development of the brain. In the collective unconscious, we see the common primal experience of humanity. In it, 'archetypes ' often appear: the birth, the death, the power, the hero, the child, God, the devil, the old man, mother earth, the moon, the sun, the wind, rivers, fire, animals and also many man-made objects such as rings and weapons. They are used in all cultures and art forms.

Diaspora or dispersion: Here meant for the Jewish people, after the Babylonian captivity and revolt against the Romans in 99-70 A.D. After 70, almost all Jews would have been expelled from present-day Israel.

DNA molecule: is composed of 4 types of nucleotides. The sequence of nucleotides is a code that records hereditary characteristics. A number of nucleotides form a gene.

Ecosystem: cooperating set of living things that thus sustain each other.

Gene: part of a DNA molecule responsible for one hereditary trait.

Hominids: humanoids. Today, modern humans are the only living species of the hominids

Mass extinction: mass destruction of a species

Mutation: change of the stable DNA when passed on to offspring

Noosphere: sphere, shell, casing of action and influence of man on earth. This term is derived from the Greek word noes, meaning mind, spirit

Organism: living being

Polymer: molecule whose 'backbone' is a long chain of carbon or silicon atoms.

Primates: gorillas, humanoids, chimpanzees, orang-utans, bonobos and some extinct groups.

System: group of organs that take care of the same function or task. For example, your stomach, intestines… have the function of digesting the food. Together, they form the digestive system.

Teleportation: is the transfer from A to B without 'physically' traversing the space between A and B. You simply disappear at spot A and reappear at spot B in zero seconds.

Geological Time Scale

EON	ERA	PERIOD	MILLIONS OF YEARS AGO	KEY EVENTS
Phanerozoic	Caenozoic	Quaternary	1.6	Humans evolve
		Tertiary		
	Mesozoic	Cretaceous	138	Extinction of Dinosaurs
		Jurassic		
		Triassic		
	Paleaozoic	Permian	240	Permian mass extinction
		Carboniferous	330	
		Devonian	410	
		Silurian		Invertebrates become common
		Ordovician		
		Cambrian	500	
Proterozoic		Also known as Precambrian		
Archean			3500	
Hadean				Earliest life

Bibliography

The phenomenon of man. Pierre Teilhard de Chardin.

Life on the edge. The coming of age of quantum biology. Jim Al Khalili and Johnjoe McFadden. An overview of the latest discoveries: how quantum mechanical phenomena influence and guide many life processes.

The layered religion. About mythical stories and critical atheists. Lucas Catherine. A scientific view of the common ground of the world's religions.

Consciousness beyond life. **The science of the near-death experience.** Pim van Lommel. Our consciousness does not always coincide with brain functions. It can even be experienced separate from the body.

The elegant universe: superstrings, hidden dimensions, and the quest for the ultimate theory. Brian Greene. An overview of all modern string theories.

Memories, dreams, reflections. An autobiography. Carl Gustav Jung.

The pagan Christ: **recovering the lost light.** Tom Harpur. The link between Christianity and the Egyptian religion.

The laws of creative evolution. José Thomas Zeberio

I have gratefully followed or adopted many passages from these books. The internet, of course, is also an inexhaustible source of information.

From each copy sold, 10% will benefit vzw.gedreven, the Toontjeshuis in Moerkerke, Belgium. (link on website)

For ideas, suggestions, additions, e-mail:

www.scienceandspirituality.be and

www.wetenschapenspiritualiteit.be